IMAGES
of America

HISPANICS AND LATINOS IN VALLEJO

The launching ceremony of the Polaris submarine *Mariano G. Vallejo* (SSBN 658), Mare Island's 506th ship, took place on October 23, 1965, with 18,000 spectators on the Vallejo and the Mare Island side. The Polaris submarine *Mariano G. Vallejo* was celebrated with full honors, and it even included a giant sombrero on the conning tower. The submarine was christened with a Christian Brothers' Napa Valley champagne by Patricia McGettigan, the great-great-granddaughter of General Vallejo. This ship was the only ship in the US history that was branded and keel-lay by a president. Pres. Lyndon B. Johnson pressed a button at the White House to start the keel laying on July 7, 1964. (Courtesy of the Vallejo Naval and Historical Museum.)

On the Cover: This photograph is of Los Gavilanes Charros de Vallejo during a Fourth of July parade in 1977. (Courtesy Vallejo Naval and Historical Museum.)

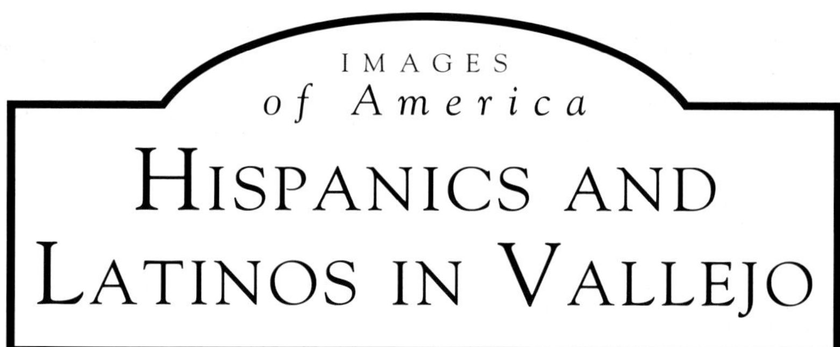

Marisela Barbosa-Cortez
Foreword by Lisette Estrella-Henderson

ISBN 978-1-4671-0774-7

Published by Arcadia Publishing
Charleston, South Carolina

Printed in the United States of America

Library of Congress Control Number: 2021948994

For all general information, please contact Arcadia Publishing:
Telephone 843-853-2070
Fax 843-853-0044
E-mail sales@arcadiapublishing.com
For customer service and orders:
Toll-Free 1-888-313-2665

Visit us on the Internet at www.arcadiapublishing.com

To my familia: parents Graciela and Israel took a big step and left everything they knew behind. To mis hermanos Sagrario, Jose y Sonia, I am so lucky to be your sister; and because of you, my childhood was fun. To my daughters Cassandra and Camelia, you are my inspiration, and to my husband, thank you for always supporting me throughout our journey.

Contents

FOREWORD

In Solano County, the city of Vallejo has the largest numbers of Hispanic and Latino residents. According to school census data, Spanish is the second most frequently spoken language in Vallejo, other than English. This statistic points to the critical importance of highlighting the contributions of Hispanics and Latinos to the historical context of Vallejo—one of the most diverse cities in California and our nation today. To effectively continue to move forward as a Hispanic and Latino community, we must take time to look back at our meaningful history established in cities such as Vallejo.

As a Latina growing up in Solano County and a longtime resident, I identify with the early Hispanic and Latino settlers of Vallejo and can relate deeply to the struggles they and their families encountered and overcame. As the first elected Latina superintendent of schools in Solano County and a lifelong educator, I fully appreciate the significance of sharing their story to learn more about their legacy, customs, opportunities, and achievements.

Beginning with Gen. Mariano Guadalupe Vallejo, who helped shape the early development of California and for whom the city of Vallejo is named, through capturing the essence of local Hispanics and immigrants as they built thriving businesses and made lasting contributions to Vallejo's success, this book highlights the many challenges Hispanics and Latinos faced when settling here. Marisela vividly chronicles the rich culture, leadership, prosperity, youth, and families of Hispanic and Latino immigrants who have influenced Vallejo's development and made it their home. Her narrative seamlessly weaves together interesting accounts of Hispanic and Latino families through prose and photographs emphasizing the importance of *familia*, *comunidad*, and *cultura* that have connected us and continue to support us throughout our lives in our pursuit of success.

I am honored to support Marisela Barbosa-Cortez as she brings to life the stories of Hispanics and Latinos in Vallejo. She is uniquely qualified to write this book having lived, raised her family, and developed her professional career in Vallejo. Her book movingly highlights that from the day they set foot in Vallejo many years ago, the Hispanic and Latino community continues to accomplish great things today!

—Lisette Estrella-Henderson
First elected Latina Solano County superintendent of schools and proud friend of the author

Acknowledgments

This book was written when anti-immigrant sentiment was growing in the United States, making it the perfect time to go back in history and reflect on how the contributions of the immigrant community helped develop the city of Vallejo. The book brings awareness of Hispanics and Latinos/Latinx contributions since the founding of the city of Vallejo. Hispanics and Latinos were anchors of this community; however, their work has been forgotten or sometimes overlooked.

Thank you to Mel Orpilla for sharing his story about writing a book on the Filipino community. At that time, I didn't think I would be writing a book about Hispanics and Latinos in Vallejo.

I would also like to express my sincere gratitude to Jim Kern, Vallejo Naval Museum executive director, for his guidance regarding using the museum's archives, research library, and photographs collections. He assisted me in making this book possible by connecting with Arcadia Publishing. Also, a big thank-you goes to Mary Kuykendall, the Vallejo Naval Museum secretary, for helping me research information and gather photographs. Thank you to Arcadia Publishing and Caroline Anderson, for your guidance.

I owe a tremendous debt of thanks to the community members of Vallejo for their willingness to share their memories that led me to research more information about Hispanics and Latinos in Vallejo: Kelly Blanco Newman, Stacie Kendrick, Esther Angel, Elaine Angel, Manuel Angel Sr., Martha Rubio, Yvonne Aragon-Armas and Jacqueline Aragon-Houston, Sandra Martinez, Lisa Wilson-Gutierrez, Dolores Ramirez-Estepa, and Pat Molinar. Thank you to all who helped me make this book possible by sharing your story either in person, Zoom, or by phone. I'm also grateful to Citlalli Flores-Zepeda and Jaime Esparza for sharing their connections and photographs.

Thank you to *mi familia*, who originally made Vallejo their home in the late 1970s. They were involved early in the transformation of Vallejo; *mis tíos* Cuca y Salvador Chavez, *tíos* Rosa y Jose Luis Segura.

Gracias to *mis padres* for taking the risk of the unknown. They left their family behind to immigrate to a new country where they had no idea what to expect, did not know the language, and all they had was hope to find a job that would provide a better life and education for their children. My mom and dad taught me that dreams do come true, and all you need is to work on them and stay focused.

Thank you to *mis hijas* Cassandra and Camelia for supporting your crazy mama, helping with the research, and accompanying me to the museum. To my husband, Roberto, thank you for your support in everything I do. You are a great father, an amazing husband, and best friend. Gracias for your constant encouragement. I love you to the moon and beyond.

Unless otherwise noted, images that appear in this book are courtesy of the Vallejo Naval and Historical Museum.

Introduction

Vallejo is well known for its naval history, waterfront, great weather, and cultural diversity. The city was named in honor of Gen. Mariano Vallejo, a Spanish descendant.

Hispanics lived in California from the mid-1700s, first under the Spanish crown and then under Mexico (1821 to 1848). The Hispanic and Latino community were instrumental in the city's establishment in the mid-1800s, shortly after California became the 31st state of the union. During this period, Portuguese and Mexicans came to Vallejo as immigrants searching for a better life, equality, and economic opportunities.

A large group of the Portuguese community came from the Azores Islands; they came to work as fishermen and dairy farmers. In 1914, the Sociedade Da Coroa Do Divino Espírito Santo built a hall serving the Portuguese community. It became a place to gather and celebrate their culture and traditions.

The Bracero program of the 1960s brought an influx of Mexican immigrants to the United States. By 1964, the city of Vallejo saw an increase in Spanish-speaking community members; as a result, people like John Aguilar and Albert Lucero began to organize, forming El Club Alegre. This organization's purpose was to gather people of Spanish-speaking descent to honor and celebrate their roots. A few years later, in 1970, the Hispanic and Latino community's presence became more potent with El Concilio Latino Americano de Vallejo; its purpose was to work together and help families in need. Sion Angel, a husband and father, was the first president of this group. The Federation of Employed Latin American Descendants Inc. (FELAD Inc.) was established in 1972 by American veterans of Mexican heritage who worked at the Mare Island Naval Shipyard. Its purpose was to address the discrimination Latinos were subjected to by the management of the shipyard. Tranquilino Martinez, activist and leader of FELAD Inc., was a key advocate for the Hispanic community in Vallejo. During this same year, Miguel Aragon founded Los Gavilanes Charros de Vallejo, bringing a stronger sense of culture with *charreadas* and participating with the local community. After being dormant since the end of the 19th century, the Hispanic business community of Vallejo saw a resurgence in the late 1950s with restaurants like Molinar's Mexico Lindo Restaurant, Casa Aragon Restaurant, and Mercado's Hair Design. In the 1980s, the first Latino market in Vallejo opened its doors, La Tapatia Market. It was not until the mid-1980s that small businesses organizations such as the Solano-Napa Hispanic Chamber of Commerce appeared. Also, during the 1990s, there was an increase in Latino-owned businesses, providing Hispanic and Latino businesses a way to organize and work together to benefit the community. The 300 to 600 block of Broadway Street is known as Little Mexico, with some of the first Latino immigrant-owned businesses such as La Tapatia Market, Bere's Bridal, and La Michoacana. Other Mexican markets are in various sectors of the city. In addition, during the mid-1980s and early 1990s, there was an influx of people from Central America, and more small businesses began to pop up, like Pupuseria Mercy and Cuban Rhythm. The 1990s and early decade of the 21st century saw an increase in the professional services business such as tax services, real estate agents, business consulting, engineering, and building contractors, to name a few.

Hispanics and Latinos are proud to honor and celebrate their roots through music and dance. A very hard-working community that values *familia, cultura, y comunidad.* It was not until the mid-2000s that more Latino organizations began to operate serving the needs of the community: Solano Aids Coalition, Diaz and Loera Centro Latino, Eric Reyes Foundation, Midsi Sanchez Foundation, El Comalito Collective, Project Blessing Bags, Green Hive, and The Time Is Ya. All of these organizations work on helping empower the Latino community.

Familia (family) is the number-one reason many Hispanics and Latinos immigrated to the United States to search for better working opportunities, better living conditions, and better education for their children. Some immigrants were forced out of their countries due to war, and many of them were separated from their families. Hispanics and Latinos arrived in different ways to cross the desert, mountains, or the Rio Grande while others came by planes or cars. The United States became the location where some were able to reunite with their loved ones. Once in this country, the families began to grow together. Some Latinos used their entrepreneurship skills to start businesses and filled a void in the community. Some of those businesses continue to operate by their descendants. Others took on the opportunity of obtaining an education and continuing to college, while others were able to secure jobs at Mare Island, the city of Vallejo, or Solano County.

Cultura (culture) Hispanics and Latinos are very proud of their native cultural heritage. While it is very diverse, it includes a blending of indigenous and Spanish colonial traditions. Since the early sixties, individuals and community organizations have shared their vibrant culture, food, events, and religious rituals; Las Posadas, Dia De Los Muertos, and Kermes, to mention some.

Communidad (community) As more immigrants move to Vallejo, Hispanics and Latinos quickly begin to understand the issues that unite them, fostering community development. They start to unite by common interests, culture, and economics. It was evident that Latinos immigrants were having difficulty fitting in Vallejo due to language and economic barriers. The founding of several clubs helped people connect and find ways to support each other, whether by assisting them in finding a job or a place to live.

Since the early 1970s, there was no elected Hispanic in the city government until Frank Castillo was appointed in 1981. It was not until 1997 that a Latina was trying to wake up the Hispanic community politically. Linda Engelman ran three times for the city council (1997, 2001, and 2003). Unfortunately, she was never elected to office. It took another nine years to have another Latina, Mina Loera-Diaz, run for office in 2012, but it was not until 2021 that the Latino community finally had representation on the city council.

The Hispanic and Latino communities are anchors of the city of Vallejo; their influence and leadership faded as time passed after the founding of the town. The influence of Hispanics and Latinos has been in a slow resurgence since the beginning of the 21st century. Only time will tell how the new generation of Hispanics and Latinos will earn their place in this city named after a successful Hispanic.

One

Beginnings

El Regalo del General

Mariano Guadalupe Vallejo was a visionary born in Monterey on July 4, 1807. By age 15, he became a cadet and quickly rose through the ranks. From 1822 to 1826, he served as personal secretary to Gov. Luis Antonio Arguello. By 1835, General Vallejo was appointed as *comandante* of the 4th Military District and director of colonization of the northern frontier. In this role, he had the authority to grant the allotment of land. General Vallejo was granted Rancho Suscol, which included areas that today are known as Vallejo and Benicia. In 1841, although prohibited by Mexican laws, Vallejo reluctantly welcomed the first American immigrants to travel overland to California. A few years later, in 1846, Vallejo was arrested in his own home by American frontiersmen. During this time, he lost most of his wealth. In 1850, Vallejo donated a five-square-mile tract of land to develop a port at Benicia and 156 acres for a state capital at Vallejo.

In Solano County, the Native American community was composed of coastal Miwok, Suisunes, Ohlone, and Patwin. Vallejo has three confirmed Native American sites located on Sulphur Springs Mountain above Blue Rock Springs Park and Glen Cove. As a colonizer, General Vallejo forced Native Americans to work for free and into Christianity and servitude. In 1837, the smallpox pandemic hit hard, and General Vallejo only focused on providing vaccinations to Californians. Many Indians lost their lives as of result of the pandemic. By 1849, he was an elected state senator advocating for the Indians' right to vote, making slavery illegal, and women's property rights, so that wives could hold separate property. The above picture is of General Vallejo with a Pomo woman around 1878. The Pomo tribe lived north of San Francisco, the Russian River, Mendocino, Clear Lake, and Sonoma Counties.

Francisca Benicia Carrillo, at age 17, married General Vallejo. She was born in San Diego to one of the most prominent California families and became the mother of 16 children, of which only 10 survived to adulthood. The city of Benicia was named after her. Doña Benicia died a year after the death of her husband in 1890.

General Vallejo and his wife, Benicia Francisco Carrillo, had 16 children; 6 died in childhood. Their daughters married, and their son Platon became a medical doctor while son Andronico taught Spanish and French. He also taught piano, flute, and vocal lessons. Andronico never married. In this photograph, Platon is in the center, and Andronico is to the left.

Capt. David G. Farragut (his original name was James Glasgow Farragut) was of Spanish descent; his father, Jorge Antonio Farragut-Mesquida, was also a US Navy officer. Farragut lost his mother due to the 1808 yellow fever epidemic. At only 9 years old, he entered the US Navy, and by age 12, he served in the War of 1812. He was the first rear admiral, vice admiral, and admiral in the US Navy. His accomplishments include serving in the Mexican-American War and being the commandant of Mare Island Naval Shipyard, which became the port for ship repairs on the west coast. In 1852, Capt. David G. Farragut was ordered to build a Navy yard by Secretary of State James C. Dobbin. The base at Mare Island that Farragut once commanded would turn out no fewer than 513 combat ships during its 142-year life, including nuclear attack submarines and the world's first aircraft carrier. Admiral Farragut owned several properties in Vallejo. The photograph is of an engraving by Gurney & Son, 1865.

One of the sons of General Vallejo and Francisca Benicia Carrillo, Platon M. Vallejo, became the first Latino native-born medical doctor in Vallejo, where he practiced from 1868 to the early 1920s. He is also known as the first California-born physician, referring to being a first-generation Latino born in the United States and the first Latino medical doctor in Vallejo. Dr. Platon became an assistant surgeon to the Navy and ships surgeon to Pacific Mail Steamship Co. Dr. Platon enjoyed the history and languages of Suisun Indians. As a young boy, he had a personal servant who was a Native American. He practiced medicine in Vallejo for 55 years.

Dr. Platon's home was located at 420 Carolina Street. He became a well-known physician serving Vallejo and its surroundings. People described him as someone that had a big heart and passion for helping others. The home is still standing. While growing up, he had some refer to him as a companion, others a servant, a Suisun Indian. Dr. Platon learned from him their customs and the Patwin dialect. This picture was taken in 1877 outside Carolina Street.

This photograph of Dr. Platon Vallejo was taken inside his Vallejo Home. He practiced medicine in Vallejo until his retirement in the 1920s. Dr. Platon enjoyed history, and in 1914, he wrote a narrative of events that took place. He died in June 1925 and was buried at St. Vincent Ferrer Cemetery. He was a devoted member of the church for 62 years, was mentored by a Dominican priest, and requested to be buried in a Dominican robe.

On August 19, 1855, St. Vincent Ferrer became the first Catholic church in Vallejo. The church was consecrated by the Dominican order of Archbishop Joseph Sadoc Alemany, OP, and Fr. Francis Sadoc Vilarra, OP. This building was originally located near the corner of Capitol and Marin Streets. The land was donated by Epifania de Guadalupe Vallejo's husband, John Frisbie.

Under the leadership of Rev. John Louis Daniel, OP, the church was moved to a new location. The chairman of the committee recommended that "Catholic churches should everywhere be, when circumstance permit, the most elevated and conspicuous edifices as the repositories here on earth of those divine truths and mysteries," and so, in April 1867, the construction of the church on Florida street began. The old church was moved next to the new church.

In the last years, General Vallejo made a living selling water from a reserve on his home named Lachryma Montis, a Latin translation of "Chiucuyem," the name used by the Indians, which means mountain tears. This picture is of Vallejo on the front porch of Lachryma Montis.

Richard Raoul Empáran (1885–1948) was General Vallejo's grandson and became the curator of the Lachryma Montis. In 1933, Lachryma Montis was acquired by the state to protect and preserve this historic site. Today, it is part of the Sonoma State Park and can be visited daily. The Vallejo family documented their history and wrote a book titled *The Vallejos of California.*

Two

Hispanic and Latinos Immigrants

Venimos A Trabajar

Portuguese community members of the Sociedade Portuguesa Rainha Santa Isabel (SPRSI) gathered for a picnic in 1906. The photograph was taken in front of the Blue Rock Springs Hotel. In the mid-19th century, Portuguese immigrants began to arrive working as fishermen, and by the early 1900s, many became involved in dairy farming (ranching). By 1913, they established the Sociedade Da Coroa Do Divino Espírito Santo (SCDES). The Portuguese settlement pattern within California concurrently began to change as they turned to the northern coastline, San Joaquin Valley, and Southern California rather than the Central Coast. Additionally, their role in the state's dairy industry steadily increased over the decades.

Joseph Miranda (originally named Jose Miranda, born in Praia de Vitória on the island of Terceira in the Azores) immigrated in 1914 at when he was 16 years old. He came to Vallejo with his brother Manuel in search of a better life. He worked seven years to earn enough money to send his girlfriend to come here to live with him. This photograph was taken on Joseph and Mary Miranda's wedding date in 1921. (Courtesy of Lisa Gutierrez-Wilson.)

Pictured below is the Miranda family in 1938. In 1916, Joseph worked for Manuel Azevedo, and he earned $40 a month. By 1939, he worked for the Sperry Mill as a shipping clerk and made $1,513 per month, which helped support his family. (Courtesy of Lisa Gutierrez-Wilson.)

The Mirandas are pictured in front of their home at 402 Amador Street, which they purchased for $1,100 from a family friend. Lisa Wilson-Gutierrez shared that his grandfather tricked his now-wife into believing that life in America was great. He borrowed a nice suit and took a picture in front of a friend's car. He sent her the picture, asking her to come and marry him. To her surprise, when she arrived, there was no car and no fancy clothes. Regardless, their marriage lasted for 64 years. (Courtesy of Lisa Gutierrez-Wilson.)

In 1922, the Sperry Flour Company located at 790 Derr Street in south Vallejo produced 5,000 barrels of flour per day, double the size of the Stockton Union Mills, which could process half that much. The mill's location on the bay made it possible to ship from Sacramento and San Joaquin Rivers by barge. The mill closed on December 3, 2004.

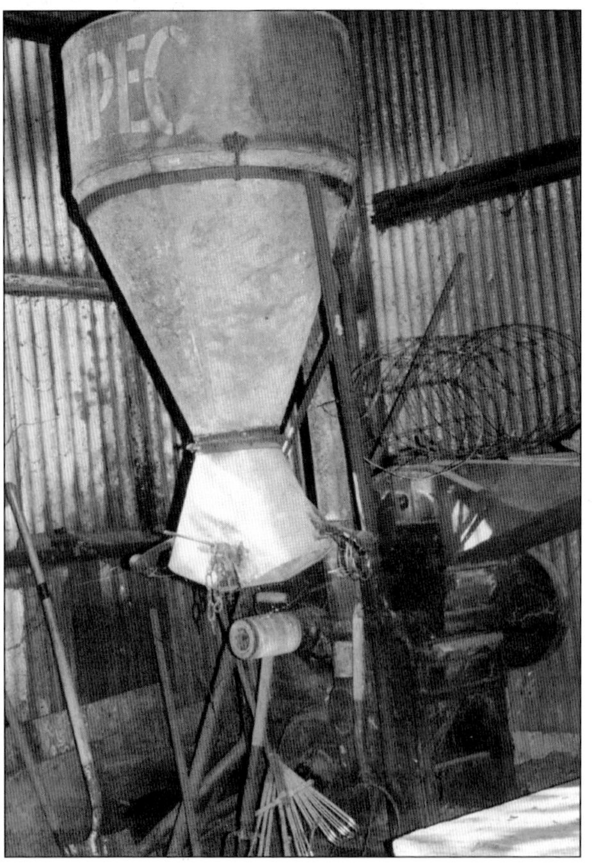

At one time, Vallejo was a "ranch town." The city had cattle, sheep, and dairy operations as well as grain and hay harvest. The Azevedo Dairy plant, located on Lake Herman Road, was the original Clyde Drake Ranch run by Joseph M. Azevedo and Maria do Rosario B. Azevedo from 1872 to the late 1960s. During the 1880s, only five percent of Portuguese immigrants were engaged in dairy ownership or labor, but by the early 1930s, this number had increased to 80 percent. After World War II, the immigration pattern changed nationwide as new Portuguese immigrants settled in cities rather than rural communities and throughout the country, rather than California. Both photographs were taken in the early 1990s.

Pictured here in 1973 at age 19 is Peggy Anne Borges, who won the Miss Dairy queen contest. She's the daughter of Mr. and Mrs. Joseph Borges, owners of the Borges Ranch located in northeastern Vallejo. Joseph Borges was a well-known dairyman and raised heifers and beef cattle.

In August 1975, Ronaldo Azevedo was 46 years old when he was appointed to fill the position of Solano County recorder. Ronaldo served in the records office for 15 years as an assistant recorder. Sadly, in June 1975, the recorder position was left vacant by the death of Ray Duvall. Ronald Azevedo was appointed for three and a half years. In 1978, he decided to seek reelection.

The Sociedade Da Coroa Do Divino Espírito Santo acquired land to build a hall, which was completed in 1915. Key leaders of the Portuguese community and UPEC (Unioa Portugueza do Estado da California) Council No. 73 provided funding to start the building. The hall was built with two floors, one for sopas and the upper for dancing the *chamarritas* (a type of music from the Azores). When this hall was built, it was a little different from others. It had a theater-style stage with an altar behind the curtain. This hall at 242 Contra Costa Street is still serving the Portuguese community and is available for rent.

S. P. R. S. I. and U. P. E. C.

Cordially invites you to attend their

First Annual Ball

S. C. D. E. S. Hall, Saturday Evening, June 4, 1932

Semi Formal

Music by Bab's Band — Dancing 9 to 1

Gentlemen $1.00 — Ladies 25c

Please present invitation at the door

This is an invitation for the first annual ball in 1932 hosted by the Sociedade Portuguesa Rainha Santa Isabel (SPRSI) and UPEC, a Portuguese fraternal society. SPRSI was established in Vallejo in 1909 as Council No. 81. The men's division of the Portuguese Society uses the initials SCDES (Society of the Crown of the Divine Holy Ghost), which was established in 1913. The purpose is to raise money for charity.

Vallejo's annual religious festival of the Holy Ghost dates to 1913 when the incorporation of Sociedade Da Coroa Do Divino Espírito Santo. The festival honors Queen Isabel, whom the community took as their patron saint. According to the story, Queen Isabel hid bread in her garment to feed the poor. She was confronted by her husband, King Dinis of Portugal, asking her to reveal what she was carrying in the folds of her dress. Upon unfolding her dress, the bread was converted to flowers. She died in 1336 and was canonized in 1625. At her canonization, she became known as St. Elizabeth of Portugal. This picture is of the 1991 Holy Ghost parade in Vallejo, with Queen Ann Ducan on the front of the SCDES.

Children and youth play an essential role during the Holy Ghost celebrations, and young Rhiannon Hamblin is the maid for the Vallejo baby queen. Her mother and grandmother are putting the final touches on her wardrobe. This event has helped the Portuguese community to embrace and stay connected with their roots. It brings the Portuguese community from several cities together to celebrate.

The first Festa do Divino Espírito (Holy Ghost Celebration), took place in 1913 in Vallejo. Since there was no hall, they celebrated at the library located in South Vallejo. This annual celebration continues the tradition with a parade, mass, and a meal. This picture from 1991 was taken during the parade in which young children carry an oversized rosary, and a girl carries the cross.

This photograph was taken in 1991 while Portuguese Society men were preparing the traditional meal, bread soaked in the juice of slow-cooked beef.

The Holy Ghost Celebration brought together the Portuguese community and provided a taste of Portuguese heritage with their traditional Sopa Festas Do Divino Espírito Santo. In this picture from 1991, Altino Tavares serves soup to guests during the 78th Festa celebration.

The first Blanco to arrive in Vallejo was Frank Antonio, born in New York City in 1854. By 1885, he and his family moved to Vallejo. Frank was a cabinet maker and eventually employed at Mare Island Naval Yard. He also donated his labor in helping to construct a portion of St. Vincent Ferrer Catholic Church. Eventually, Frank became Vallejo's first probation officer and served as a truant officer for the public schools. When apprehended, the students were taken to J.P. Utter's office in the Lincoln Grammar School for reprimand. (Courtesy of Kelly Blanco Newman and Stacie Kendrick.)

The Blanco family is pictured here. From left to right are (seated) Frank A. Blanco Sr., Morton Blanco, Ramon Blanco, Mary "Mae" Blanco, and Mary Valentine Harlow Blanco; (standing) Tony Blanco, Frank A. Blanco, Edwin Blanco, and George Blanco. Edwin became a city commissioner, Antonio Joseph became a football player with the Winged V's, and Ramon became a banker living in Beverly Hills. (Courtesy of Kelly Blanco Newman and Stacie Kendrick.)

Eddie W. Martinez was a fifth-generation Californian and native of Vallejo. A graduate of Vallejo High School in 1928, he began his career at Mare Island Naval Shipyard as an apprentice rigger. On July 7, 1964, Martinez was the master mechanic service group and chairman of the keel-laying committee for the *Mariano G. Vallejo* (SSBN 658).

Sus Rives, a Native Vallejoan of Puerto Rican descent, was well known in high school for his sprinter speed and worked at Mare Island. He was an active member of the Federation of Employed Latin American Descendants and a supporter of the Latino community. He helped people fill out paperwork and provided any support when language was a barrier. The community describes him as a very giving and honest person.

Joseph Sandoval was the president of Metal Trades Council at Mare Island Naval Shipyard. In 1983, he became the president of the Federation of Employed Latin American Descendants.

In 1974 during "Awareness Week," a meeting was held with a panel discussion for shipyard personnel to become familiar with local and state vocational programs for recruitment. The luncheon took place at Mare Island Officers Club. Joseph Sandoval, seated in the center, was the chairman of the Equal Employment Advisory Committee.

Solano County, rich in agriculture, was a destination for migrant workers. In 1942–1964, the Mexican Farm Labor program established the Bracero Program, allowing Mexican farm laborers to work in the United States. The Mexican Farm Labor Agreement with Mexico guaranteed decent living conditions and 30¢ per hour for each employee. In addition, a private savings account was created in Mexico, where part of the money was sent. As of 2021, the braceros still alive have not received any of their savings from the Mexican government. In Vallejo, Spanish-speaking (primarily Mexican) immigrants began to arrive in the late 1950s and early 1960s. Latino residents in Vallejo worked in various fields: agriculture, factories, seamstress, laborer, concrete, landscape, and housekeeping.

In 1974, the park and building maintenance staff of the Greater Vallejo Recreation District (GVRD) pose for a picture to show off their new uniforms. The GVRD had a diverse group of employees.

In 1964, Maria Romero Sanchez, from Cuernavaca, Mexico, was an exchange teacher for Vallejo Junior and Vallejo Senior High school. She is pictured here on January 27, 1964, while teaching 11th grade at Vallejo Senior High School. Sanchez was the "Lady of Honor" during the Vallejo Rotary Club's Ladies' Day meeting.

Mariana Molinar, known as "Martha," was the manager of Molinar's Mexico Lindo Restaurant. This 1977 photograph shows the dolls she was preparing to give away to poor children in Tijuana. Martha previously owned businesses in Tulare and Rodeo. When she moved with her son and his family to Vallejo, Martha, a vital part of Molinar's Mexico Lindo Restaurant, was a dedicated businesswoman.

Sion and Esther Angel immigrated to Vallejo in the 1960s from Mixtlan, Jalisco, Mexico. Sion worked for Bill Maher & Sons (now known as Strange and Chalmers) for over 20 years and retired in 1982. Initially, life in Vallejo was not easy; he and his wife, Esther, had difficulty finding a place to rent when they first arrived. Sion was the first *presidente* of Concilio Latino Americano de Vallejo. Sion Angel passed away in 2007. (Courtesy of Esther Angel.)

Salvador Chavez and his wife, Cuca, immigrated to Vallejo in November 1964 from La Estancia, located in the municipality of Tamazula de Gordiano in the Mexican state of Jalisco. They raised their five children—Raul, Arcelia, Salvador, Leticia, and Alicia—in Vallejo. Salvador mentioned that one of the reasons for joining El Concilio was because the purpose was to help the community, and it was not business-related. He recalled El Concilio donated funds to help victims of the 1985 Mexico earthquake. Salvador and Cuca were very active members of El Concilio Latino Americano de Vallejo, and as of October 2021, they are the last surviving married couple of El Concilio. (Courtesy of Alicia Chavez-Penner.)

Three

Community Leaders

Somos Agentes de Cambio

Edwin J. Blanco was born and raised in Vallejo. He was a St. Vincent's School graduate and operated his blacksmith shop at the exact location Tuff Lawrence Tavern was located in 1956. His political life started in 1921 by serving two years as city commissioner of public health and safety as an interim appointment. During office, the police department installed one of the first radios systems in the United States. Edwin is also given credit for Vallejo's first pension system for the police and firefighters. In addition, the fire department was expanded, and the No. 2 fire station was built, located on Alameda Street. (Courtesy of Kelly Blanco Newman and Stacie Kendrick.)

Edwin Blanco was a blacksmith until he was hired as a chipper and caulker at Mare Island Navy Yard. (Courtesy of Kelly Blanco Newman and Stacie Kendrick.)

Edwin J. Blanco was an animal lover and horse shoer specializing in race horses. He was also a breeder and exhibitor of purebred dogs and English game bantams. Even after he became commissioner of public health and safety, he enjoyed raising prize poultry and, in 1937, captured 20 prizes at the California State Fair in Sacramento with his entry of 21 birds. Edwin was an International Kennel Club judge and fisherman. (Courtesy of Kelly Blanco Newman and Stacie Kendrick.)

Edwin J. Blanco was at the christening of the USS *California* at Mare Island. In 1932, while he was still commissioner, he established his own insurance business at 1713 Sutter Street. He continued to operate it until 1948, when his son-in-law Ambrose Boyle entered a partnership with him. The same year he opened his insurance agency, he was appointed state inheritance tax appraiser by controller Ray L. Riley. He served in that capacity for 23 years, including time under controllers Thomas H. Kuchel and Robert Kirkwood.

The Winged V's football team pose for a photograph in 1906. The Vallejo Winged V's were an amateur football team that, during a short period of six years, won 65 games, lost 1, tied 3, and dominated their competition throughout California. Antonio Joseph Blanco was a member of this team, and Ray Blanco was the mascot.

This chair belonged to Dr. Platon Vallejo and is now in the home of Stacie Kendrick, great-granddaughter of Edwin J. Blanco. Stacie shared the story that Frank Blanco saw six chairs outside the house of Dr. Platon ready to be thrown in the trash, so he asked if he could have them. The chairs originally were upholstered with leather, but the family decided to reupholster and hand embroider them due to wear and tear.

Eddie W. Martinez, a fifth-generation Californian and native of Vallejo, is pictured here. A graduate of Vallejo High School in 1928, he began his career at Mare Island Naval Shipyard as an apprentice rigger. On July 7, 1964, Martinez was the master mechanic service group and chairman, keel laying committee for the *Mariano G. Vallejo* (SSBN 658). He served on the Vallejo City Council from 1967 to 1971, two of those years as vice mayor.

Eddie W. Martinez was the recipient of the Civilian Service Award presented on behalf of the secretary of the Navy in 1945. He was the youngest Mare Island master of the shipyard's Shop 72. A proud veteran, Martinez served on active duty in Japan during the Korean Conflict. In 1971, he retired as service group superintendent with 43 years of federal service; he also retired from the US Naval Reserve with the rank of commander.

Pictured here is Tranquilino Joseph Aduelo Martinez de Jimenez-Mendoza, a disabled veteran. He grew up as a hardworking farm laborer in the valleys of Texas and Central California. His father migrated to San Francisco in 1941 to work as a welder at the shipyards. Tranquilino joined the California Army National Guard in 1953. He was honorably discharged on July 15, 1954, and enlisted into the US Navy on July 16, 1954. He was then honorably discharged on July 18, 1960, with the rank of petty officer third class and appointed as the Hispanic employment program manager for the Equal Employment Opportunity Program for the Mare Island Naval Shipyard in 1967. Tranquilino was very proud of his work with the Federation of Employed Latin American Descendants (FELAD). One of the incidents he is most proud of is La Clinica Ole in Rutherford, California, in 1972. The Napa Board of Supervisors wanted the clinic closed due to building issues concerns. The *clinica* director, Tala de Winters, asked FELAD Inc. for help. So the organization stepped in and addressed the county board, questioning the improper requirements and deadlines. La Clinica Ole continues to operate today.

Tranquilino is pictured celebrating Hispanic Heritage Week at Mare Island in 1969. Hispanic Heritage Week became official under Pres. Lyndon Johnson in 1968 and was later expanded to a one-month celebration by Pres. Ronald Reagan in 1988. Its purpose is to celebrate the history, culture, and contributions of Spanish and Latin-American descendants. As director for FELAD, Tranquilino served on numerous boards and committees, such as the affirmative action committee for Vallejo schools; housing, employment, and health boards; and other committees.

In 1971, Sus Rives (far right), pictured with his wife Evangelina, baby son Juan Carlos, and stepson Victor, dealt with an immigration issue. Sus was advocating for his wife have to have immigration paperwork to be handled in the United States. Still, immigration law required that they go to Mexico to finalize all documentation.

In 1960, Mutual Fund Associates, Inc. announced the appointment of Filomeno A. Gonzales, a graduate of the University of California. Filomeno moved to Vallejo in 1955 and worked for Pacific Vegetable Oil Corporation Del Sur.

Frank Castillo was a CBS/KCBS account executive and community advocate. Earlier in his life, he was a pathfinder in the Air Force during World War II. His appointment to the city council was after the death of councilman John Cunningham in 1981. He ran for office but lost the election. In this picture, he is with members of the Imagination Car Club. He helped them secure a rental space when they were denied because the receptionist thought they were gangsters.

Coco Corona, a Mexican native raised in Sacramento, moved to Vallejo in 1988. By 1991, Corona was the first woman elected to be president of the Solano-Napa Hispanic Chamber of Commerce. She was a businesswoman and an expert in the area of public relations and owner of By Design Multimedia. In 1993, Corona led the efforts as a member of Latino Task Force, a community organization under the umbrella of Fighting Back Partnership, and coordinated Festival de Familias (family festival), a two-day event to celebrate and showcase Vallejo's local culture and provide alcohol-, drug-, and violence-free activities for the community. The event took place behind the city hall on July 3, 1993.

Claudia Quintana Salvadoran immigrated to California when she was 11 years, but it was not until 1999 that she moved to Vallejo. Claudia became the first Latina and female city attorney to serve the city of Vallejo. Quintana worked with Solano County public defender's office and then as assistant city attorney before becoming the Vallejo city attorney. She retired after serving eight years as Vallejo's city attorney. As of 2021, she works for Legal Services for Children, helping children obtain their legal status. (Courtesy of Claudia Quintana.)

Roberto Cortez, a native of El Salvador, made Vallejo his home in 1990 after graduating from college with an engineering degree. He became an active community member by volunteering with St. Vincent's Ferrer Catholic Church Spanish-speaking youth group. In 2009, he was elected president of the Solano Hispanic Chamber of Commerce. In 2012, he was appointed to the City of Vallejo Planning Commission and the Governance Committee of the Workers Compensation Insurance Rating Bureau of California, serving 2016–2021. He currently is part of the City of Vallejo permit appeals board. Roberto is an engineer who has received and been recognized by several organizations for his commitment to support local businesses and nonprofit organizations. The photograph is from the 2010 Hispanic Business Salute Award gala. (Courtesy of Roberto Cortez.)

Pictured here is Marisela Barbosa-Cortez, a first-generation immigrant. In 2010, she was president of the Solano Hispanic Chamber of Commerce. In 2013, she was appointed to the First Five Solano County Commission, and in 2017, she became the seventh woman to chair the Vallejo Chamber of Commerce and the first Latina in the 142nd year in the chamber's history. This image shows Marisela taking the oath of office administered by Erin Hannigan-Andrews, County Board of Supervisors District 1. Also in the photograph are Jenny Tsang (left) and Richard Curtola, chamber of commerce president and CEO from 2010 to 2016. (Courtesy of Kristian Medina.)

Carlos E. Solorzano-Cuadra immigrated from Nicaragua to New York in 1969 and has been an active member of the business community since 1988. He is a veteran of the US Marine Corps who served during the Vietnam Era. Carlos worked many jobs, from a dishwasher, janitor, waiter, to computer programmer. In 1991, he helped organize the Black Chamber of Commerce and the Filipino American Chamber of Commerce. His dedication and the ability to work with diverse segments of the business community have been invaluable tools to develop his business and serve the community. (Courtesy of Carlos E. Solorzano-Cuadra.)

Originally from the Bay Area and partially raised in El Salvador, Roxana Damas made Vallejo her home in 2016. Roxana is a strong advocate in the areas of human rights, gender, and domestic violence prevention. In 2016, she was selected as one of 170 women to represent Empower Women Champions sponsored by the United Nations. Roxana is an artist and community advocate. (Courtesy of Roxana Damas.)

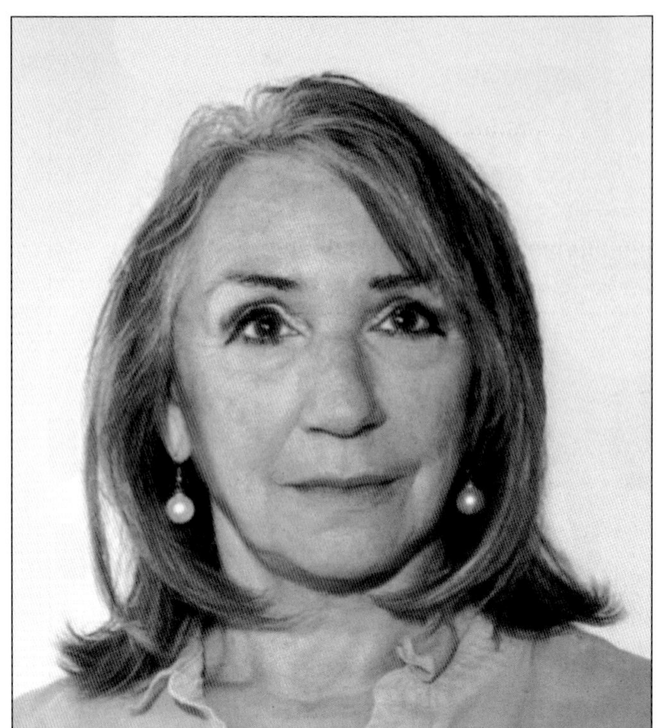

Christina "Tina" Arriola was born and raised in South Vallejo. A board member and membership coordinator of the Mira Theatre Guild, she was also a board member of the Vallejo Community Arts Foundation. In 2021, she was sworn in as the first District 6 city council member and the first native-born Hispanic woman for that district. (Courtesy of Christina Arriola.)

Louis Alexander Matias is of Dominican descent and ran for the city council in 2020 as an Afro-Latino who saw the need for better representation in the city government. He lost the election for District 1 but as of 2021 continues his commitment to the Vallejo community by serving on the Economic Vitality Commission and Code Enforcement Appeals Board. (Courtesy of L. Alexander Matias.)

Mina Loera-Diaz, An immigrant from Ojocaliente, Calvillo Aguascalientes, Mexico, came to the United States at five years old. Her dad, Antonio Loera, was part of the Bracero Program, and by the age of 17, she made Vallejo her home. Mina is a retired employment specialist for Contra Costa County Employment & Human Services Department. In 2007, she founded Diaz and Loera Centro Latino, a nonprofit organization to provide bilingual, multi-service volunteer community organizations designed to meet the needs of Latino families. Mina partnered with Vallejo Unified School District, Solano County Mental Health, and the Vallejo Police Department through the organization. She ran for the city council in 2016 and did not receive enough votes to win the election. As a resident of Vallejo, her goal was to bring a fresh voice to the council and run again in the 2020 election. In 2021, Mina Loera-Diaz was sworn in as the first Latina, first immigrant, and first District 1 city council member. Mina is the first Latina to hold such a position in Vallejo. (Courtesy of Mina Loera-Diaz.)

Robert Briseño was born and raised in Vallejo. While in college joined the Army Reserves and earned a commission as an officer. He served in the Army Reserves for over 11 years in finance, military police, and adjutant general units and became airborne qualified. He is a local magazine business owner and the 2021 chairperson of the Greater Vallejo Recreation District Board of Directors. This is a picture of Roberto with his wife, Regina. (Courtesy of Robert Briseño.)

Manuel Angel, a native of Vallejo, graduated from Vallejo High school and obtained a college degree from Academy of Art University with a bachelor's degree field of study cinematography and film/video production serves as the digital marketing coordinator for Visit Vallejo. He was appointed to the Solano County Fairgrounds Board of Directors in 2018. Currently, he is the chairman of the board. (Courtesy of Manuel Angel.)

Omar Martinez, a former combat medic and owner of Pupusería Mercys, became the captain of the Vallejo Guardian Angels in 2009. The volunteer organization worked primarily to discourage crime elements by being a visual deterrent, and members were trained in verbal conflict resolution. The organization became known as the Solano County Guardian Angels. Omar also founded the Bay Area Street Safety Patrol. Omar was recognized as the "Spirit of Solano" by the Solano Hispanic Chamber of Commerce and the Filipino American Chamber of Commerce.

In 2019, Natalie Ramos became the first Latina valedictorian in the Jesse Bethel High School. She is a first-generation American of Mexican and Salvadoran parents. There was some controversy about her being chosen as valedictorian, and her mother took it to social media: "My daughter Natalie is ranked No. 1 in her class with a 4.27 GPA. She was told by her counselor that she would be the first Latina Valedictorian at Jesse Bethel High School, and it seems like the Principal has a problem with that. Principal Cusi wants her to share the spot with nine other students. This has never been done before at Jesse Bethel; why now? The moment a Latina becomes Valedictorian, it seems to be a problem." The school had to review their handbook, which stated that the valedictorian is "the student with the highest weighted academic GPA 9–12 in academic classes from 9th grade through the first semester of senior year will be chosen the Valedictorian for the class." Jesse Bethel High School had to update the GPA calculations, and in fact, Natalie Ramos met the criteria. Natalie is currently attending the University of Berkeley. (Courtesy of Natalie Ramos.)

Four

BUSINESSES

SOMOS UNA FUERZA EMPRESARIAL

Pictured are Martha Molinar and her son Adam F. Molinar in front of their restaurant Molinar's Mexico Lindo on 802 Sonoma Boulevard. The restaurant first opened in May 1958 with afternoon operating hours of 2:00 p.m. to 10:00 p.m. Martha cooked, and Adam assisted while still working full-time at Selby Smelting Co. near Crockett, California. Despite a permit challenge from the City of Vallejo, the restaurant opened. (Courtesy of Pat Molinar-Jeffers.)

Molinar's Mexico Lindo Restaurant is one of the first Mexican restaurants in Vallejo, operated by Adam F. Molinar and his family for 45 years. The restaurant was best known for its delicious tostadas. It also received national recognition from *Gourmet* magazine on September 9, 1972. Adam worked at Mare Island as a general foreman in Ship 56 while still handling the financial decisions of the restaurant. In the 1960s, the restaurant relocated to 541 Benicia Road. The restaurant had a trendy display of piñatas, *zarapes*, and jewelry from Tijuana. Due to the popularity of Mexican items at the restaurant, the Molinars saw another opportunity and decided to open Molinar's Imports on the 300 block of Georgia Street. Rachel Molinar, Adam's wife, operated this business for five years, and then they added the imports to the restaurant. (Courtesy of Pat Molinar-Jeffers.)

Pat Molinar, at 12 years old, did as her parents and grandmother told them. All of the children helped in the day-to-day operation of the restaurant. Pat recalls that "in the 1960s, a lot of things had to be introduced. People love the guacamole on the chip, and we were known for the tostadas and its sweet sauce. Dad was community-oriented, and family was his number-one priority. I don't know how he did it, but he always had time for us." (Courtesy of Pat Molinar-Jeffers.)

Molinar's Mexico Lindo Restaurant was not only known for its authentic Mexican food but also for its ambiance. The second restaurant was ethnically decorated and also had live music. Their most popular dishes were the tostadas, chile verde, and chile relleno. The restaurant provided a way to keep Martha employed and bring in additional income for the family. Adam Molinar was known for sponsoring several local organizations such as Vallejo Little League, Babe Ruth Pal Soccer, motocross, and adult valley sports. In 1978, Adam and his wife, Rachel, seen in this picture, are very happy to be celebrating Molinar's Mexico Lindo's 20th anniversary.

Mexico Lindo is beautifully decorated with items bought in Tijuana. Meals were prepared fresh, including freshly made flour tortillas and salad dressings. The restaurant included a gift shop, and on weekends, customers were entertained with music.

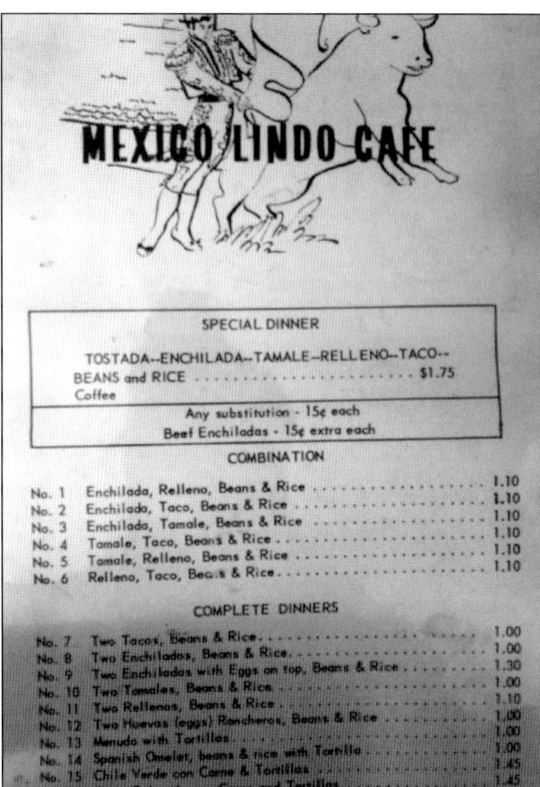

MEXICO LINDO CAFE

SPECIAL DINNER

TOSTADA--ENCHILADA--TAMALE--RELLENO--TACO--
BEANS and RICE $1.75
Coffee

Any substitution - 15¢ each
Beef Enchiladas - 15¢ extra each

COMBINATION

No. 1	Enchilada, Relleno, Beans & Rice	1.10
No. 2	Enchilada, Taco, Beans & Rice	1.10
No. 3	Enchilada, Tamale, Beans & Rice	1.10
No. 4	Tamale, Taco, Beans & Rice	1.10
No. 5	Tamale, Relleno, Beans & Rice	1.10
No. 6	Relleno, Taco, Beans & Rice	1.10

COMPLETE DINNERS

No. 7	Two Tacos, Beans & Rice	1.00
No. 8	Two Enchiladas, Beans & Rice	1.00
No. 9	Two Enchiladas with Eggs on top, Beans & Rice	1.30
No. 10	Two Tamales, Beans & Rice	1.00
No. 11	Two Rellenos, Beans & Rice	1.10
No. 12	Two Huevos (eggs) Rancheros, Beans & Rice	1.00
No. 13	Menudo with Tortillas	1.00
No. 14	Spanish Omelet, beans & rice with Tortilla	1.00
No. 15	Chile Verde con Carne & Tortillas	1.45
No. 16	Chile Colorado con Carne and Tortillas	1.45

Pictured here is a Molinar's Mexico Lindo original menu from when the restaurant was known as a cafe. (Courtesy of Pat Molinar-Jeffers.)

Gonzalez Restaurant first opened its doors in Vallejo in 1977 and closed in 2020. It was one of the oldest operating restaurants in Vallejo. This photograph is from January 1981. Dona and Gerri (at right) were the winners of the Name the Grande Platter Contest. They submitted "Ay Chihuahua," and they won! Luiz Gonzalez is pictured on the left.

The photograph is of the grand opening day, September 1, 1977, of Mercados Hair Design, one of the oldest Hispanic own beauty salons located on Tuolumne Street. The owner was Esther Mercado, and the business was well known in the community.

Manuel's Auto Body shop opened in 1983 to do collision repair. After graduation, Manuel learned the art of body fender repair, and he loved it. A few years later, he was hired as an interim instructor to teach auto body shop classes at Solano Community College. Manuel was given a special temporary accreditation to teach a semester. He is one of the best in the auto body shop business. (Courtesy of Manuel Angel.)

The first Mexican grocery store in Vallejo was La Tapatia Market, established in 1982 at 1083 Sonoma Boulevard. Ismael Magallanes and his brother Ignacio "Nacho" Magallanes operated the store. This small market brought Mexican food and served the community of Vallejo during a time in which the Latino community was growing in Vallejo. The 1990 picture shows Ismael in his store.

In 1996, the Magallanes brothers opened their current location on 601 Broadway Street, as a much bigger store that now includes foods from Central and South America and Mexican apparel and piñatas. In addition, to groceries, La Tapatia Market has a *carniceria* and a small restaurant. It continues to be in operation by Ismael and his brother Ignacio Magallanes. (Courtesy of Roberto Cortez.)

Jaime and Leticia Vargas opened their grocery store in 2001. Jaime worked in construction as a heavy machine operator while his wife and family operated the store. The store includes a *carniceria* and restaurant offering freshly made tacos, tamales, and pollo asado. The store is located on the north side of Vallejo, serving the Latino community primarily on the border of American Canyon. The store was designed by professional engineer Roberto Cortez and built by Joel Angel of JA Angel Contruction. (Courtesy of Roberto Cortez.)

Owned and operated by Hector Chavez, Guanajuato Market opened in 2002 at 14 Laurel Street. The store is located on the south side of Vallejo and serves a large immigrant community. The store is the closest to this neighborhood and within walking distance of local families. Then Chavez opened Market Guanajuato Grill Deli at 1652 Fairgrounds Drive. In the last few years, it has expanded to providing central and Latin-American food. Its second location on the northwest side of Vallejo primarily serves the Central American community. (Courtesy of Marisela Barbosa-Cortez.)

Mariza Alcazar and Ubaldo opened La Michoacana paleteria y pasteleria in 2006. They venture to show their kids that as Latinos, they could make their dream possible. One of the challenges of their business was the permit. The planning department had a big concern about the *paletas* wrapped in plastic and the garbage it would produce, assuming that people will throw plastic back on the street and clog the drainage system. (Courtesy of Marisela Barbosa-Cortez.)

Bere's Bridal is owned and operated by Maria Sanchez and Carmela Sandoval. They opened in 2001 after noticing a need for formal wear almost 30 years ago. In 2017, they were recognized by Congressman Mike Thompson with the American Dream Award. Both ladies are great supporters of the Vallejo community. For years, they have been working with Vallejo Together to help provide resources to homeless people and Diaz and Loero Centro Latino. During Christmas, they host Las Posadas (Christmas celebration) for underserved children.

Tortilleria Pinto was started by Humberto "Pinto" Lobato and his wife, Elizabeth Cervantes, in 2001. It is the only *tortilleria* (place that sells freshly made tortillas) in Vallejo that provides fresh tortillas, tamales, fruits, and vegetables. Humberto passed away in early 2021, and now the store is operated by Elizabeth and her six children. (Courtesy of Marisela Barbosa-Cortez.)

La Rosa Market originally opened in 1997 as Dulceria La Rosa No. 2 on 448 Georgia Street. Edgar Jimenez and his wife, Delia, first focused on a candy store in Vallejo but quickly realized there was another need for produce and food in downtown Vallejo. Edgar, originally from Mixtlan, Jalisco, Mexico, immigrated to California in 1988 and moved to Vallejo when he opened his store. In 2003, the couple had an excellent opportunity to move La Rosa Market to its current location on 738 Sonoma Boulevard. The family has operated the store since its beginnings. As of 2021, La Rosa continues to fill a void in an underserved community. The current location has parking, and in addition to meats, produce, and deli items, the store is known for its traditional Mexican food: tacos, *pozole*, *menudo*, and *birria*. This store has become essential due to the lack of grocery stores in South Vallejo. (Courtesy of Marisela Barbosa.)

Tacos Jalisco started as a taco truck restaurant, and due to its success, owner Martha Rubio decided they needed a larger space. Currently located at 3420 Sonoma Boulevard, Tacos Jalisco is the oldest operating Mexican restaurant in town. The success of Tacos Jalisco was delicious tacos and salsas. It also helped that it opened at a time when the Vallejo Latino population was increasing. Martha mentions that part of her success was the Vallejo High School students: "They bought our food and spread the word among their parents, family, and friends." This photograph was taken in April 2021 while the business community was operating under COVID-19 pandemic guidelines. (Courtesy of Marisela Barbosa-Cortez.)

Gloria Kulik, a native of El Salvador, founded Azteca Business Services in January 1990. She focuses on providing business and personal tax services for the Vallejo Latino community. She was also a member of the Solano-Napa Hispanic Chamber of Commerce. (Courtesy of Roberto Cortez.)

Salon de Belleza Diva's (Beauty Salon Diva's) is owned and operated by Dolores (Lolis) Lugo and Erika Gonzalez since the early 2000s. The salon is located at 330 Broadway Street, part of the Little Mexico neighborhood. This beauty salon is well known for being a good place where clients get excellent services and are treated nicely. They have accommodating hours of operation that align with the Latino-market needs.

El Nopal had been operated by a husband-wife team since 1986. Jose Lopez and his wife run it; their food is freshly made and authentically Mexican. The COVID-19 pandemic hit the business community hard, and as of December 2021 there was a note on the door informing customers that it would open again soon. (Courtesy of Roberto Cortez.)

Street vendors began to appear in Vallejo in the mid-2000s, usually at critical locations throughout the city and often moving around various neighborhoods at designated time frames. Typically, a cart is equipped to provide fruit cups, *elotes*, *mangonadas*, and other easy to-go foods. It has also become more common to see them walking throughout neighborhoods and selling their goodies, similar to small towns in Latin America. This photograph is from spring 2021.

In 2020, there were 17 taco truck stations throughout the city of Vallejo. Since the 1960s, *loncheras* have existed, but it was not until the 1970s that taco trucks began to pop up in Los Angeles. One of the first taco trucks that appeared in Vallejo was Tacos Jalisco, in the 1980s. By the early 2000s, the business community was divided about having food trucks around town. The Solano Hispanic Chamber of Commerce got involved by helping the trucks stay and serve the Vallejo community. This photograph is from 2020, and the taco truck has a permanent location in the parking lot of Billar Los Portales.

Pupusería & Taquería Mercy is owned and operated by Omar Martinez. The restaurant opened its doors in 1988. The photograph was from the early 1990s, when the restaurant was located on 1414 Sacramento Street. Due to a fire, it relocated to 333 Tennessee Street. This is the first Salvadoran restaurant in Vallejo. Pupusas are small, round-like pancakes made with cornflour (masa) and filled with cheese and beans or meat (pork). (Courtesy of Omar Martinez.)

Pupusería & Taquería Mercy relocated to 333 Tennessee Street due to a fire. The restaurant has added a store that sells traditional Salvadoran soccer jerseys, flags, and many other items.

Little Maya Bakery was the first Latino-owned bakery in Vallejo. It opened its doors in the mid-1990s and quickly became known for its delicious tres leches cakes and freshly made Mexican bread. (Courtesy of Roberto Cortez.)

Manuel Melendrez immigrated from Mexico to the United States in 1973. His chef skills were obtained while working at the Hyatt Regency Hotel. In 2012, he opened Momo's Cafe, known for its great American and Mexican food, good portion serving sizes, and location in up-and-coming downtown Vallejo. (Courtesy of Roberto Cortez.)

For Latinos, appearance is essential, and jewelry adds pride. Leticia Delgadillo, owner of Alexis Jewelry and Princess Imports, first opened her shop's door on Georgia Street in 2003 in downtown Vallejo. As a result of the growing demand for bridal, christening, and formal wear, the shop relocated to 923 Tennessee Street and added Alexis Formal Bridal and Alexis Jewelry. During Christmas, the shop sponsors a posada for the community. (Courtesy of Roberto Cortez.)

Jewelry Gallo De Oro is located in downtown Vallejo. The store has been family operated since 1986. The photograph shows Christopher Hernandez (left) with his dad and brother working on a Saturday afternoon in the summer of 2021.

Monarch Engineers was founded in 2006 as a civil and structural engineering company serving the bay area. Today, Monarch Engineers provides local and international multi-disciplinary engineering and design services with a niche in special events. The company has been the engineer of record for several notable events such as Super Bowl 50, the 34th America's Cup, and SailGP around the world. (Courtesy of Roberto Cortez.)

Pictured here is Pat Molinar, daughter of Adam and Molinar, the owners of Molinar's Mexico Lindo Restaurant. Pat was in the banking industry for 16 years, and in 2006, she became a realtor. She is married to Stuart M. Jeffers and has a son, Stuart P. Jeffers, and daughter, Veronica C. Jeffers. (Courtesy of Pat Molinar-Jeffers.)

Luis Romero immigrated to the United States in 1981 at 14 years old after his father's death in El Salvador. During his first year at Vallejo High School, Luis was placed in an English as a second language class, where he ended up assisting the teacher. At one point, he was told not to speak Spanish because people would look down on him. Luis found a need for Spanish-speaking realtors, and in 1991, he became a realtor and continues to serve his community. (Courtesy of Luis Romero.)

Five

Nonprofit Organizations

Apoyando A Nuestra Comunidad

Club Alegre De Vallejo was founded in 1964 as a social club and identified as a "Spanish" or "Mexican" club with the purpose to connect Spanish-speaking people. Pictured on February 5, 1972, is the installation of officers. From left to right are Mrs. Louis Munoz, secretary; Joe Alfaro, president; Mary C. Nevarez, vice president; Joseph Vincente, installing officer; Victor Nevarez and Shuy Vazquez, trustees; and queen Alice Saltado. Meetings were held monthly in members' homes.

This photograph from 1976 was taken during the installation of El Club Alegre officers. From left to right are Ben Ortega, president; Julia Vasquez, secretary; and Les Childers, vice president. Childers took several photographs of the Hispanic community.

This picture was taken on September 18, 1969, and El Grupo Alegre De Vallejo used it to promote their event "Night in Mexico" from 6:30 p.m. to 1:00 a.m. at St. Vincent's Memorial Center. The entertainment included "La Shispita" Berta Alicia Leanos, a child singer star from Mexico; a Mariachi California group, and dancing music by Connie Caudillo.

One of the traditions of being a queen is making sure that she has the proper attire, and a cape was very important at all coronations. To be a contestant, the young girls needed to be of Mexican descent and between the ages of 16 and 19. The coronation dance took place in September of the same year. On May 16, 1970, El Club Alegre hosted a yearly queen contest. The contestant that sold the most tickets is the winner, announced at the June dance. The cape was an essential part of their outfit. One of the duties of the El Club Alegre queen is to participate in a float in the Fourth of July parade.

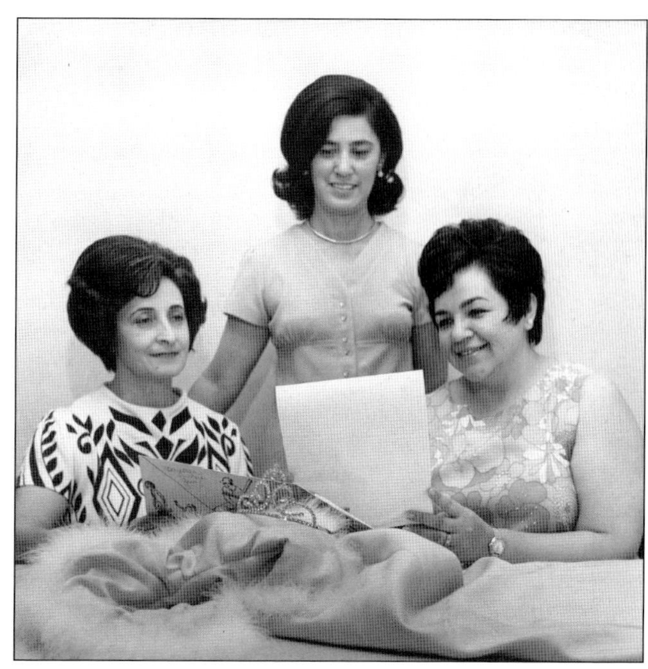

The outgoing queen of El Club Alegre De Vallejo crowns her successor, Annie Perez, during the coronation ball on September 22, 1972. This event had 400 attendees, just like the big 10th-anniversary celebration at Dan Foley Cultural Center, with a theme to honor past queens. By 1977, the dance celebrations were taking place at McCormack Hall on the Solano County Fairgrounds.

Since El Club Alegre was a social club, it had events throughout the year. This December 23, 1970, photograph shows the planning committee focused on publicity, dance, and decorations for the New Year's party celebration. The club always had noisemakers and party favors for the special evening. The committee members seen here are, from left to right, Mrs. Heins, Mary Nevarez, and Mrs. Aguilar.

On May 17, 1973, Bertha Padilla, a student at Vallejo High School and a volunteer at Kaiser Permanente Hospital, was awarded a $100 scholarship; she planned to attend California State University at Hayward to major in nursing. Jesus Vasquez, president of the club, presented the scholarship.

El Club Alegre also participated in the Fourth of July parade with highly decorated floats. The queen had to be part of the float; these photographs are from the 1975 parade. Similar to other clubs, volunteers spend hours designing and decorating the float.

This photograph was taken on January 26, 1973. Concilio Latino Americano De Vallejo was the second oldest service organization in Vallejo, composed of Spanish American, Mexican American, and Mexican immigrants. Esther Angel shared that the group began organizing through the church by helping remodel the small church on Sonoma Boulevard and Lemon Street, St. Louis Bertrand. The members not only raised funds for material but also helped with the actual work. Under the guidance of Rev. Saturnino Mujica and Rev. Patrick O'Regan, they could organize and plan the group's activities. They also formed a Spanish choir. One of their goals was to unite and serve families of Mexican and Latino descent.

The 1977 board of directors installation, El Concilio Latino Americano de Vallejo, focused on helping the community and providing a way for newcomers to connect with other Spanish-speaking people in Vallejo. During the 1970s, all local clubs created similar banners to the one pictured here.

This picture is of the 1976 board of directors El Concilio Latino Americano de Vallejo installation dinner. The board had a dress code for board members. Some of the male directors wore a similar burgundy suit or just a burgundy blazer with gray pants during the installation, along with a matching tie. The women wore white dresses or outfits with a similar tone.

To fundraise the most money possible, they also had *rifas* (drawings) on the day of the event. The items include televisions, cash, radios, and others. In this picture, Cuca Chavez (left) assists the queen with the raffle tickets. (Courtesy of Salvador and Cuca Chavez.)

Similar to El Club Alegre de Vallejo, El Concilio Latino Americano de Vallejo also had a queen contest. In this photograph, Mrs. Saldivar holds her creation made of burgundy red velvet and taffeta lining. The difference in style from other clubs is demonstrated by lace and rhinestone edging. This photograph was taken on May 3, 1972.

Salvador Chavez and his wife, Cuca, seen here with the queen, were active members of El Concilio Latino Americano de Vallejo and participated in all events. They dedicated a lot of their time to the organization and made long-lasting friendships through it. (Courtesy of Salvador and Cuca Chavez.)

This image was captured on November 22, 1975, during the fifth-year celebration of Concilio Latino Americano De Vallejo, which took place at Dan Foley Cultural Center. Sion Angel, on the left, was the first president of El Concilio Latino Americano de Vallejo in 1970; next to him is his wife, Esther Angel, followed by Alice and Joe Vincenty. The organization formed a choir, provided citizenship classes, celebrated Cinco de Mayo, hosted Las Posadas, founded Piñata Day, provided assistance to needy people by donating food baskets, and had a scholarship fund. It also published a bilingual newsletter.

Seen here in 1977, the Fourth of July was a yearly event in which El Concilio Latino Americano de Vallejo enjoyed participating. Group members dedicated several hours working together to develop an idea for the float and then making the float. Cuca Chavez recalls using tissue to make the flowers, and then the men helped decorate the car. The "Vallejo, All-American City" float won first place in class one of the parade.

The queen was also required to participate in the Fourth of July parade. After the parade, the members celebrated in the park or at the waterfront for the rest of the day. "It was a family fun day for all the members," said Salvador Chavez. After the parade, the club members and their families gathered at Blue Rock Springs park to have a potluck-style picnic. (Courtesy of Salvador and Cuca Chavez.)

El Concilio Latino Americano de Vallejo organizes a yearly posada. During this event, several other organizations joined the celebration. The tradition of a posada is to reenact Joseph's and Mary's journey to Bethlehem. The Mexican tradition includes songs, meals, and piñatas. In Vallejo, the celebrations take place at people's homes, and the person hosting is responsible for providing the dinner or snacks. In 1972, the Las Posadas tradition was started by Alice and Joe Vincenty, natives of Mexico City, to share their traditions with the Vallejo community. This picture was taken at the home of Mrs. Alfaro (standing at the front door). Mr. and Mrs. Lupe Casillas (holding the statues of Joseph and Mary) and young girl Tanya Culver are asking for shelter.

In the photograph to the left, Jennie Padilla and Julia Abeyta hold statutes representing Joseph and Mary to role play and sing the traditional songs. In the photograph below, Dominga Trujillo led the attendees to pray the rosary, part of the Las Posadas celebration during December 1980.

On December 28, 1972, El Concilio Latino Americano de Vallejo hosted a Christmas party at St. Vincent's School cafeteria, also known as a Mexican posada. From left to right are Mrs. John Briceno and her son Richard, Rosita Barragan (dressed as an angel), and Mrs. Alberto Sanchez.

This picture is from December 28, 1972, during a Las Posadas celebration. In this photograph, young Peter Palacios Jr. is ready to break the piñata as people sing a song. Carmen Abeyta is holding the piñata, and the young girl is Lisa Pena.

On December 23, 1973, while El Concilio Latino Americano De Vallejo focused on honoring and celebrating Mexican and Latino traditions, the organization also incorporated American traditions. They held a well-attended annual Christmas party (about 200) guests. Some of the board members made the event more festive by dressing up. Santa Claus handed out gifts to attendees. From left to right are Kate Abeyta Jan Ortiz, and Julia Abetya, dressed as reindeer, with Ray and Linda Campos as Mr. and Mrs. Claus.

Cinco de Mayo celebration for El Concilio Latino Americano de Vallejo was a big fundraising event. They held their annual coronation ball at the Dan Foley Cultural Center. The money raised helped fund the scholarship program, and each year, the funding disbursement was bigger. The first scholarship was $100, and by the 1990s, it was $500. This picture, from June 1973, shows the scholarship recipients. Pictured from left to right are (first row) Teresa Abeyta from Hogan Senior High School, Madelen Torres from St. Vincent's High School; (second row) Anthony Rillera from Vallejo Senior High School, and James Sandoval from St. Patrick's High School.

Los Gavilanes was a Mexican association founded in 1972 by Miguel Benito Aragon, Manuel Bustos, and Miguel Chappell. They brought the Mexican Charreria culture to Vallejo. They had *ezcaramuzas* (female equestrian event in the Mexican charrería) and *charreadas* (similar to a rodeo) in Solano County and throughout California. They traveled to Mexico to participate in special events. (Courtesy of Jacqueline Aragon-Houston and Yvonne Aragon-Armas.)

Los Gavilanes had an annual Mexican rodeo in May, usually held at the Solano County Fairgrounds. Candidates for charro queen were presented to the public and chosen by a panel of judges. To be a contestant, the young lady needed to be between the ages of 14 to 18, speak Spanish, know how to ride a horse or be willing to learn, and live in Vallejo. Lucero Hope was the first charra queen in 1972. (Courtesy of Jacqueline Aragon-Houston and Yvonne Aragon-Armas.)

Los Gavilanes de Vallejo was the idea of Miguel Aragón, a Mexican American native of New Mexico that moved to Vallejo in 1958. He spent 12 years in the marines and shared a passion for animals. Through Los Gavilanes, Miguel wanted to share with people the authentic Mexican culture. He leased the land of what he called "Rancho de los Gavilanes." (Courtesy of Jacqueline Aragon-Houston and Yvonne Aragon-Armas.)

During that time, the beer in style was Olympia and Coors, which sponsor most of the events. Part of Miguel Aragón's job for the day was to advertise the beer among attendees. The photograph was taken at Los Gavilanes Ranch in 1979. (Courtesy of Yvonne and Jacqueline Aragon-Houston.)

Miguel Aragón's daughters participated in *charrerías* as part of the *ezcaramuzas*. A *charrería* is a Mexican rodeo where charros and charras showcase their abilities. Los Gavilanes brought big competitions to Solano and other parts of the state. (Courtesy of Yvonne and Jacqueline Aragon-Houston.)

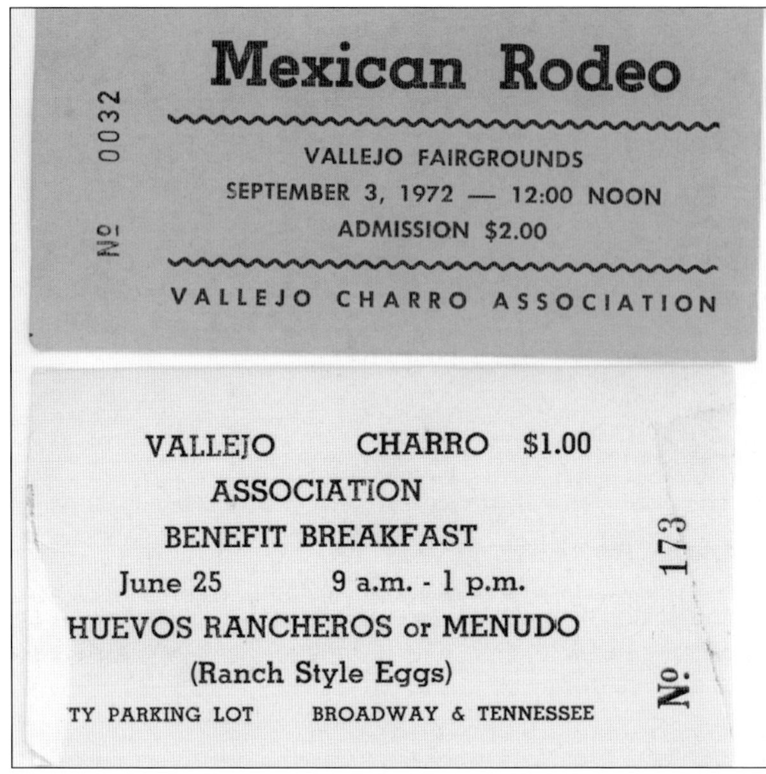

Mexican Rodeo
№ 0032
VALLEJO FAIRGROUNDS
SEPTEMBER 3, 1972 — 12:00 NOON
ADMISSION $2.00
VALLEJO CHARRO ASSOCIATION
VALLEJO CHARRO $1.00
ASSOCIATION
BENEFIT BREAKFAST
June 25 9 a.m. - 1 p.m.
HUEVOS RANCHEROS or MENUDO
(Ranch Style Eggs)
TY PARKING LOT BROADWAY & TENNESSEE
№ 173

Los Gavilanes *charreadas* brought people from all over the bay area, and events could draw up to 500 attendees. This is a photograph of the tickets for the Mexican rodeo in 1972. The rodeo was for educational purposes and to share the Mexican culture with the community. The benefit breakfast was hosted at Casa Aragon Restaurant on Broadway and Tennessee Street. (Courtesy of Yvonne and Jacqueline Aragon-Houston.)

HOTEL TRAVELERS
Have a

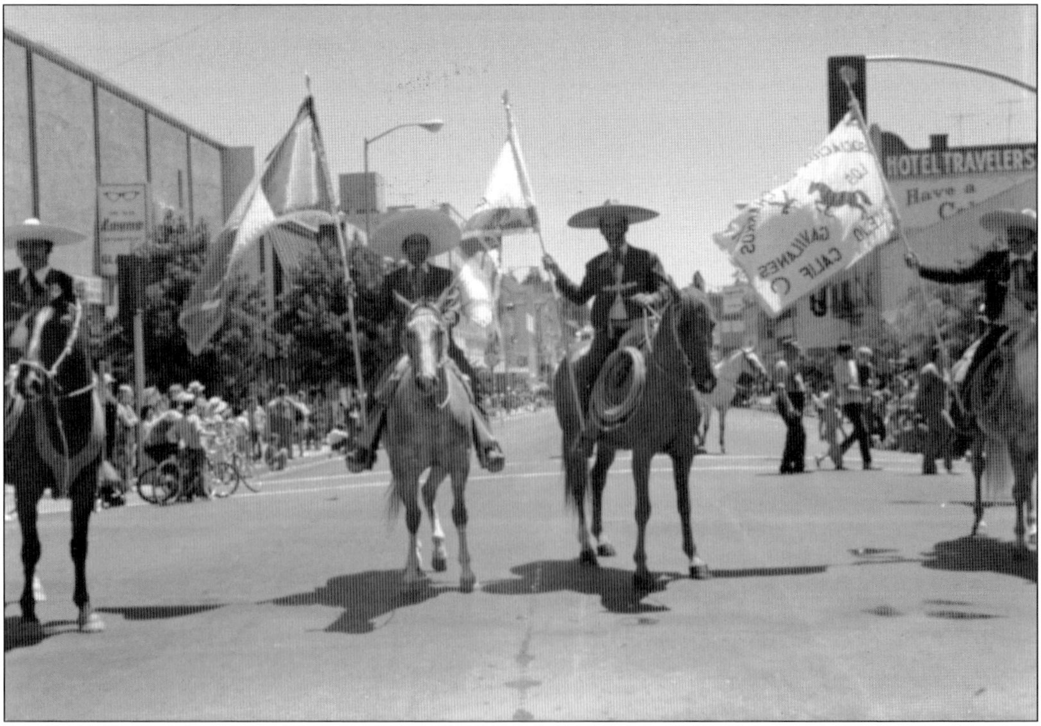

In 1975, when FELAD was planning Un Baile de Primavera, Sus Rives was the master of ceremonies. Dances were a way to fundraise money to help people that did not qualify for government agency aid. By the mid-1970s, a branch of FELAD was formed called FELAD IMAGE, and a much-younger dance committee was in charge of organizing the dance.

On February 25, 1975, a group of leaders composed of several local organizations, such as FELAD and ROCA (Raza Organized College Awareness), plans the day-long event, which will start with a parade, mariachi, luncheon, and conclude with a dance in the Fairfield Civic Center.

In August 1975, members of the Federation of Employees of Latin American Descent dress up to advertise the Baile de Agosto, an August dance at McCormack Hall on the fairgrounds. The dance included a one-hour performance from the Napa Folklorico de Napa Colegio. Los Buhos provided dancing music.

Ruben Abundis, originally from Los Angeles, moved to Vallejo in 1966 and, as a retired Mare Island machinist, set on a mission to help Latinos find and develop artistic skills. FELAD launched a Youth Art Alliance pilot program. This was possible due to a grant by Pacific Telesis Foundation. FELAD's goal was to reach young Latinos between the ages of 10 and 19 years that were either high risk or had an art interest. Ruben's interest in art started when he was 10 years old. FELAD continue to provide activities for youth until the early 2000s.

The Guadalupana Association of St. Basil's Church was formed in 1971 by a group of Hispanic parishioners dedicated to honoring and promoting devotion to Our Lady of Guadalupe. The group had 30 members in 1971. This portrait of Our Lady of Guadalupe was presented to St. Basil's Parish on January 1, 14, 1971.

The Guadalupana Association held an annual bazaar and awarded a TV set as a door prize. Kathy Torres accepted the award on behalf of her father, Joseph Torres.

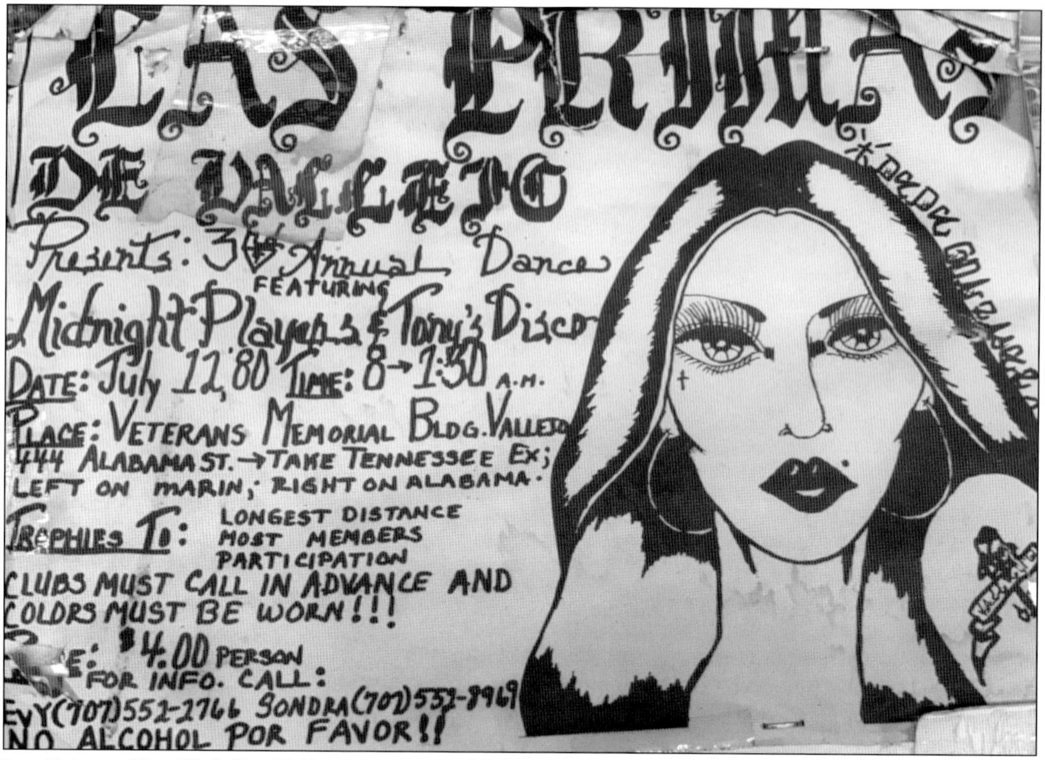

LAS PRIMAS
DE VALLEJO
Presents: 3rd Annual Dance
FEATURING
Midnight Players & Tony's Disco
DATE: July 12, '80 TIME: 8→1:30 A.M.
PLACE: VETERANS MEMORIAL BLDG. VALLEJO
444 ALABAMA ST. → TAKE TENNESSEE EX; LEFT ON MARIN; RIGHT ON ALABAMA.
TROPHIES TO: LONGEST DISTANCE
MOST MEMBERS
PARTICIPATION
CLUBS MUST CALL IN ADVANCE AND COLORS MUST BE WORN!!!
$4.00 PERSON
FOR INFO. CALL:
EVY (707) 552-2766 SONDRA
NO ALCOHOL POR FAVOR!!

Las Primas Car Club De Vallejo was started by a group of young women interested in cars. The original founders were Evy Gonzalez, Lizliz Gonzalez, Rafaela, Gonzalez, Rita Garcia, Elaine Alvarez, Diane Sanchez, Debbie Sanchez, Marriane Sanchez, Margaret Jaramillo, Maryann Jaramillo, Rosie Diaz, Dolores Ramirez, Sondra Ortega (vice president), Tynia Ortega, and Petra Carrillo. They began to host annual dances in 1978. The purpose of the dance was to get together and enjoy each other company. Pictured above is a handmade ticket for the annual dance. The photograph below shows original members of Las Primas car club. (Both, courtesy of Dolores Ramirez-Estepa.)

Dolores Ramirez-Estepa wears her car club jacket in the photograph to the right. She was one of the original founding members of the club. Dolores is of Filipina and Mexican descent. In the September 2021 image below, she is pictured with her car during a Vtown Car Club reunion, where she helped by providing food for the homeless community. (Both, courtesy of Roberto Cortez.)

Imaginations Car Club participates in the Fourth of July parade. In the 1970s, the club was run by Gilbert Salgado, Pete Dizon, Manuel Angel, Fernando Diaz, Roberto Diaz, Jaime Diaz, and the Delarosa brothers. Gilbert Salgado was the first president, and Manuel Angel, the second president. Manuel became very active with the community. Imaginations Car Club was born out of a love of building cars and pride in cruising the vehicles down the street. The young men spend hours working on their vehicles; however, people had a bad image. It was assumed that they were part of a gang and were constantly harassed by the police. (Courtesy of Manuel Angel.)

Manuel Angel (on the left) was the second president of Imaginations, and he decided to become more community involved so the people were aware of the Imaginations Car Club's actions. They started food drives and raising and donating money to the Special Olympics. The club's image changed, and Manuel was nominated for awards, including the Junior Chamber of Commerce award. The club's activism altered the perception of the Latino club, and the members felt proud of their accomplishments. The club had about 30 members. (Courtesy of Manuel Angel.)

One of the reasons Imaginations started to participate in local events was to be known by the community. The Fourth of July parade was a great way to showcase the members' cars. In the photograph is Manuel Angel, president of Imaginations Car Club and Ballet Folklórico de Aztlan. The car is a 1966 Chevy Impala owned by Gerardo Angel.

Imaginations Car Club hosted fundraising events with performances from members. The funds raised from the event were donated to the Special Olympics. (Courtesy of Manuel Angel.)

This truck features the words "SACRIFICIO," meaning sacrifice. On top of the truck are the awards won during a car show. (Courtesy of Manuel Angel.)

Carlos Trevino and Susie Sturgeon, in 1988, started the Solano Hispanic Chamber of Commerce. By 1989, it officially filed the proper documentation to be a chamber of commerce. The first board of directors was elected Carlos R. Guiterrez, president; Maria Kennedy, vice president; Manuel Cosme, treasurer; Susie Sturgeon, secretary; and Carlos Trevino, board director. While in infancy, the board decided to grow by incorporating Napa, and the chamber became known as the Solano-Napa Chamber of Commerce. After several years, the two separated, and the Hispanic Chamber of Commerce of Solano County continues its activities throughout Solano. The Hispanic Chamber of Commerce has presidents from Vallejo and throughout Solano County.

In this image, Vallejo business community leaders meet to discuss issues affecting the community. Coco Corona, Solano Hispanic Chamber of Commerce president, speaks with Hermi Sunga, president of the Filipino American Chamber of Commerce, and James Phelps, president of the African American Business Network. In 2004, the Vallejo Business Alliance was formed to promote communication and collaboration among all Vallejo Chambers of Commerce. As of 2021, the committee is known as the Vallejo Chambers Alliance.

It became customary for the Vallejo Business Alliance to be part of the Fourth of July parade. The four chambers of commerce participated in the Vallejo Fourth of July parade. The 2010 president of the Solano Hispanic Chamber of Commerce and her family participated in the parade. The picture is from the 2010 parade. (Courtesy of Roberto Cortez.)

Mario Saucedo, the founder of Solano Aids Coalition, has helped families affected by HIV serve the community for the last 20 years. The organization focuses on education and prevention programs. Saucedo said, "I want to be involved with our Latino community to bring the community together." Saucedo moved to Vallejo from Los Angeles; he worked as a special effects artist and custom designer for 20 years. Saucedo lost all of his friends due to the HIV pandemic, so he decided to open a thrift store to help those dealing with HIV. In addition, he wanted to provide education and condoms, so the Solano Aids Coalition was born in 2002. (Courtesy of Roberto Cortez.)

Dia de Los Muertos is traditionally only celebrated in a church; however, if one lives in Mexico, they will be honoring the dead in the cemetery. In Vallejo, it was first observed by Mario Saucedo in 2004. Saucedo is the founder of Solano Aids Coalition and set out to create and build a stronger community by using his artistic talents and Mexican roots. Creating *las catrinas* (tall female skeleton wearing fancy dresses and hats, the most recognizable symbols of the Day of the Dead), showcasing them during a parade, and having community members create altars was the best way to incorporate the many aspects of Dia de Los Muertos. (Courtesy of Jaime Esperza.)

In 2019, the Latino community in Vallejo was in full force, registering new voters. This photograph was taken during Dia de Los Muertos in downtown Vallejo.

Mina Loera-Diaz founded Diaz & Loera Centro Latino in 2014. It is a bilingual, multi-service volunteer organization designed to meet the needs of Latino families. Mina started by offering various services: free translation services, citizenship workshops, tutoring, and parent educational support. The organization is operated by volunteers from Vallejo and throughout Solano County. The workshops are hosted by Bere's Bridal at its Broadway Street location. In addition, the organization focus on outreach for the Spanish-speaking community. In 2020, during the COVID-19 pandemic, there was also an increase in fires in California. Diaz & Loera Centro Latino prioritize disaster awareness community outreach. In this picture on the left, Lisa Guiterrez-Wilson helps Mina Diaz-Loera (right) share information with the community. (Courtesy of Mina Loera- Diaz.)

In collaboration with the Stanford Office of Community Engagement, the Solano County Public and Green Hive, a nonprofit organization, formed a mental health wellness group. They met to discuss issues and concerns impacting the community to tackle a problem and provide a solution. The group conversation was bilingual. This picture is from one of the meetings that took place in fall 2019. (Courtesy of Green Hive.)

Green Hive, located in downtown Vallejo, has been working with the Metropolitan Transportation Commission since 2015. Marisela Barbosa, the founder of Green Hive, is a community-based consultant and helps engage the Latino community. This picture is from a community focus group that took place in 2018. (Courtesy of Green Hive.)

The Eric Reyes Foundation was started by his mother, Isabel Reyes, to honor the memory of her son, who was taken away due to a senseless act of violence on February 6, 2016. Reyes was on his way to graduating with a 4.0 grade point average, and all he dreamed of was going to college Sadly, Reyes was shot to death, making him the second homicide in Vallejo. The photograph was Reyes's high school senior picture. (Courtesy of Isabel Reyes.)

Eric Reyes and his mother, Isabel, took this picture at their home in 2015. The first thing on Isabel's mind was to get guns off the street, so she founded the Eric Reyes Foundation, with a mission to engage youth and provide education resources to help them achieve their academic potential. Isabel started by contacting the Vallejo Police department and asking for assistance to create a gun buyback program. In 2018, she hosted the First Annual Hispanic Heritage Celebration, "Remember Me," to honor her son and provide scholarships for high school students. She also partnered with Franklin Middle School and offered after-school tutoring services. (Courtesy of Isabel Reyes.)

In 2014, the "Women of Influence" event was hosted by two Latinas: Liz Ramos and Marisela Barbosa. The event's purpose was to have an opportunity for an open dialogue about how women have succeeded in their career paths. Women from Vallejo and Solano County attended the event, and part of the proceeds was donated to Soroptimist International of Vallejo. From left to right Alma Hernandez and Ramos. (Courtesy of Alma Hernandez.)

On November 15, 2018, Touro University hosted California's inaugural Community Lamplighter Awards. The award recognizes leaders in the area of health, education, community, and social justice. The proceeds from the evening are to support diverse student scholarships. The keynote speaker was Xavier Becerra, California attorney general and the first Latino to hold the office in the history of the state. In this picture, Becerra, the 33rd California attorney general from 2017 to 2021, is on the left. (Courtesy of Roberto Cortez.)

Project Blessing Bags was founded by Mildred Gains (Puerto Rican) and her husband, Craig. They began by donating items that fit in a one-gallon bag to the homeless community. Her success is to the support she receives from community members who are genuinely concerned for the homeless and underserved population. Mildred is a stronger believer in community support, and in addition to Project Blessing Bags, she volunteers her time to help other nonprofit organizations. Mildred has a full-time job as the regional executive director for PIQE (Parent Institute for Quality Education). (Courtesy of Mildred Gains.)

El Comalito Collective was founded in 2015 by Abel Rodriguez and Edgar-Arturo Camacho Gonzalez. Their art gallery and retail space provide workshops, showcasing of artwork, opportunities for historically marginalized groups to display their talents. Through the years, Abel and Edgar have been providing art classes for kids and adults, virtual painting parties, and art exhibitions, and they have filled the void of providing bilingual art classes in Vallejo. They empower the Latinx community. (Courtesy of Mina Loera-Diaz.)

Inspired to make a difference in Vallejo, The Time Is Ya began to organize in 2018 when a few Latino Leaders attended the first "It's Political" meeting scheduled due to a political and social climate that was unfriendly and to some extent hostile. Eleven people attended the first meeting and had Latinos from Vallejo, Fairfield, Suisun City, and Vacaville. The group includes business owners, community advocates, community members, and professionals. The group believed that the community had significant needs to create the force and strategies to protect the community and set goals to gain political power. By 2019, they will form a political action committee (PAC), The Time Is Ya PAC. The first photograph shows the first meeting that took place in 2018. The second photograph was of the first community bilingual forum in 2019, in partnership with community leaders and nonprofits. (Courtesy of Roberto Cortez.)

The Vallejo Naval and Historical Museum hosted "Latina Leaders of Solano County" during the Women's History Month with a panel discussion featuring four past presidents of the Solano County Hispanic Chamber of Commerce: Marisela Barbosa-Cortez, Karla Paz-Prieto, Andrea Canola Garcia, and Doriss Panduro. Moderated by community activist and artist Roxana Damas. The event was the idea of David Gonzalez Vallejo Naval Museum and Jim Kern, executive director of the museum. (Courtesy of Kristian Medina.)

The Solano Hispanic Chamber of Commerce offers scholarships to middle and high school students from Solano County. During the 2010 gala, six students were honored with a scholarship. To qualify for the scholarship, students needed to submit an essay. The scholarships were presented by Matt Garcia's family. (Garcia, a young councilman, was killed in Fairfield.)

Five

Art, Culture, Youth, and Family

Celebrando Nuestras Raíces, Cultura y Familia

Piñata Day Festival in 1972 was started by Concilio Latino Americano De Vallejo in partnership with the Greater Vallejo Recreation District. From left to right, (first row, seated) Ricardo Briceno and Judi Morales; (second row) Theresa Morales, Miguel Briceno, and Juanita Briceno will be performing.

This 1975 photograph was taken during the Piñata Day Festival, a collaboration of El Club Alegre and Los Gavilanes Charros. The event took place at Children's Wonderland Park and included a parade, entertainment, and activities for the kids, including making a piñata and tortillas. In this August 1975 picture are young charro Miguel Chappell, dancer Yvette Aragon, and Chris Bouger.

The Piñata Day Festival included a flour-making tortilla demonstration presented by Mrs. Minga Trujillo (center). Also pictured are (left) Larisa Cespedes and Clarisa Morales (right).

Ballet Folklórico is key to Mexican culture, and in the 1970s, Vallejo celebrated the Vallejo Ballet Center. Katina Moelk and Paula Tooliatos from the Vallejo Ballet Center performed at the Concilio Latino Americano De Vallejo event. From left to right, Jeannette Herrera and Primitivo Herrera are part of El Concilio Latino Americano de Vallejo.

In 1973, the Vallejo Charro Association "Los Gavilanes" invited the Senior Adults Social Club to the charros dance. All seniors were invited as guests of the charros. Pat Valencia presents the invitation to Ann Sitton.

The First Mexican Rodeo took place at the Solano County Fairgrounds in 1972. The event was a success, and it continued for several years. Los Gavilanes was competing throughout California and Mexico. (Courtesy of Jacqueline Aragon-Houston and Yvonne Aragon-Armas.)

Hispanic Employee Program manager Monique Kristofors and Cdr. Capt. Ernest Scheyder review the display showing the contributions of Hispanics to America prepared in honor of the Hispanic Week in September 1983.

In 1979, Mare Island celebrated its 125th anniversary. The event included various performances. Folklore dancers Marlene Rodriguez, and Joseph Garcia danced to a traditional Mexican song.

The Ballet Folklórico de Aztlan was started by Maria Escalante and Sonia Rodriguez. The dancers wear traditional dresses from Jalisco and Veracruz, Mexico. They performed at several Hispanic and Latino events as well as at the Fourth of July parade. Traditionally, the dancers were young middle and high school students. Rolena Lantoyo (pictured left) is an El Ballet Folklórico De Vallejo dancer at the youth festival. She wears the traditional dance from the State of Jalisco, Mexico.

The Dia del Niño celebration was hosted by Diaz and Loera Centro Latino on May 17, 2009. It is a big day for children to feel special in places like Mexico. The schools will host shows, music, and festivals for children to enjoy the day. In 2009, the local businesses on Broadway Street provided funds and locations to host the event. It included face painting, horseshoes, dance music, and activities for children.

Jose Luis and his wife, Rosa Segura, are pictured in traditional Jalisco attire, ready to enjoy the 2009 Dia del Niño event. Jose and Rosa helped the community when they needed translation or issues at school. In the 2000s, Jose helped organize a ballet folklórico at Vallejo High School and later participated in Sister City events. (Courtesy of Roberto Cortez.)

Dia del Niño events included performances, games, food, and charros. This little charro is learning how to rope in 2009. La Tapatia Market allowed the use of their back parking lot for the event. (Courtesy of Roberto Cortez.)

Dia de Los Muertos is traditionally only celebrated in a church. Mexican culture honors the dead in the cemetery. In Vallejo, it was first observed in 2004 by Mario Saucedo, founder of Solano Aids Coalition. (Courtesy of Jaime Esparza.)

Dia De Los Muertos *altares* (altars) are built by community members to honor the dead during the Dia de Los Muertos celebration. The decor includes traditional decorations, flowers, and food. (Courtesy of Roberto Cortez.)

This image was captured at the 2012 Solano County Fair, which takes place in Vallejo. In this picture, ballet folklórico performs at the Cultural Pavilion. The pavilion purpose is to display the cultural history, art, crafts, and entertainment for the community. There are different performances and all-day displays of Latino culture, the Inter-Tribal Council, the Filipino community, the Solano Hispanic Chamber of Commerce, and the Black Chamber of Commerce. (Courtesy of Kristian Medina.)

In this 2014 photograph is a young boy with his mother playing *Loteria* (a traditional game of chance similar to bingo but using images instead of numbers) at the Solano County Fair. Each year, a different theme was displayed; during this particular year, the Solano Hispanic Chamber of Commerce members created a childhood-game interactive table. (Courtesy of Kristian Medina.)

Quinceañeras are most heavily associated with Mexico; however, La Fiesta de Quinceañera is celebrated throughout Latino America. It celebrates the 15th birthday of the young lady and marks her transition to womanhood. It is believed that the tradition came from the indigenous Aztec and Mayan groups, and upon the arrival of the Spanish, they added the Catholic mass component, in a way to give thanks to God for reaching womanhood age. (Courtesy of Ian Thurston.)

Erica Candido is pictured with her *padrinos* Israel and Graciela Barbosa at her *quinceañera* in September 2003. *Padrinos* are part of the tradition in a *quinceañera* and tend to be family or friends that help with the event, but not necessarily. Erica had a traditional *quinceañera* mass and a big party. (Courtesy of Elba and Erica Candido.)

Sandra Portillo celebrated her birthday with a *quinceañera* in 2017. She attended many parties and enjoyed *quinceañeras* because of how unique the young ladies looked like princesses. In the photograph, she dances to the song "Morena de mi Corazon" by Los Lobos. Sandra is proud of her Salvadoran and Mexican roots. The party took place at the Filipino Community Center. (Courtesy of Sonia Portillo.)

Cassandra decided to have her *quinceañera* pictures taken in front of St. Peter's Chapel at Mare Island before her party. Her special moment was walking into the reception and seeing all her family and friends supporting her continue to mature into a young woman. (Courtesy of Ian Thurston.)

St. Peter's Chapel is the oldest naval chapel in the United States. The chapel was built in 1901 under Chaplain Adam McAlister. It features Victorian Gothic architecture, and the Tiffany stained-glass windows were installed to honor individuals and groups.

Ballet Folklórico Moon Azteca started with six members in 2015. Yajaira Rubio, originally from Sinaloa, Mexico, where she was raised until the age of 15, started the group with her three sisters, a niece, and her daughter and son. Yajaira has been dancing since she was four years old, so music and culture are her passion. Over the years, she has grown the group, and now she is known in town as the head of a great performance dance group. (Above, courtesy of Jaime Esparza; left, courtesy of Yajaira Rubio.)

Cinco de Mayo celebration on the Bere's Bridal parking lot. In addition to the festival, nonprofits participated in providing services to the Latino community. Traditional Aztec dancers are pictured here. The event was hosted by Diaz and Loera Centro Latino and Bere's Bridal. (Courtesy of Mina Loera-Diaz.)

St. Louis Bertrand is a small parish at the corner of Lemon Street and Sonoma Boulevard. Many Hispanic and Latino families met here, and Concilio Latino Americano De Vallejo was created because Latinos wanted to meet other Latinos and build a community. In the 1970s, they donated time, money, and work to make this a little nicer looking from the inside. It was here that the Spanish choir started and a Spanish youth group that helped the community by fundraising to donate food and celebrate Father's Day and Mother's Day. It was not until the 1980s that Latinos were given a space at St. Vincent's Ferrer Parish.

December 12 is a significant day for Catholic Latinos. Our Lady of Guadalupe is celebrated with *mañanitas* (Mexican birthday song) at church. Children attend mass dressed in traditional Indio and India outfits and bring flowers to Our Lady of Guadalupe. This picture is of young girls attending mass at St. Vincent Ferrer in 1986.

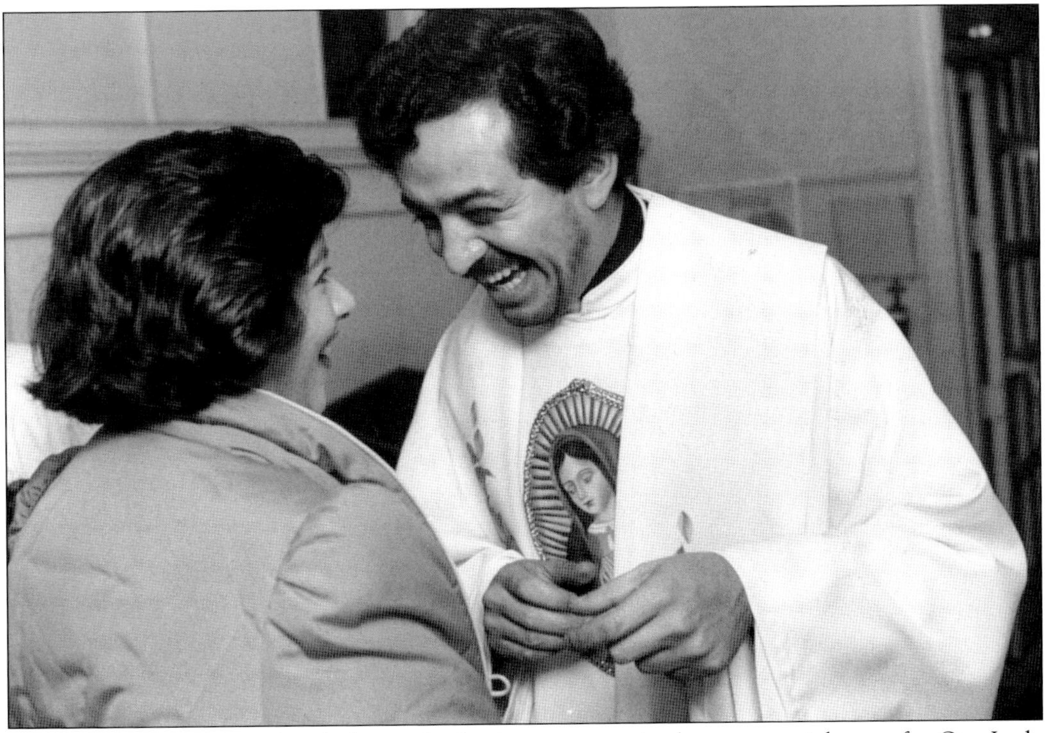

Father Jaime was critical in helping the Latino community have a special mass for Our Lady of Guadalupe at St. Vincent's Ferrer Parish in 1986. Since the early 1970s, Latinos' mass and celebrations have taken place at St. Louis Bertrand. There was always a concern about Latinos not contributing to the parish enough money. Father Jaime started by separating all the contributions made by Latinos to prove that they did contribute and that they also deserved the same privileges that other members had.

As the Latino population grew, so did the celebration for Our Lady of Guadalupe. In 2009, parishioners dedicated several hours to recreate a pilgrimage similar to what takes place in small Mexico or Latin American towns. They created a float and dressed as the Virgin Mary. They then proceeded by signing and praying to the church. (Both, courtesy of Citlalli Zepeda.)

Victory Outreach Church, since the 1990s, has increased the demand for services. The congregation welcomes Christians and those who seek to understand Christianity. Their parishioners learn following the example of Jesus. The church has been making an impact in Vallejo and advocates for at-risk youth. Jaime Magallanes discusses his past gang experiences with Pastor Dominic Cuevas in the office of Victory Outreach Church.

The Funky Aztecs are a Chicano rap group best known for collaborating with Tupac Shakur on "Slippin' Into Darkness." The group started in the 1990s with Merciless (Marco Parada), Indio (Ricardo Parada), and Sapo-Loco (Raymond Campos). Their music is a mixture of political rap and street stories. The picture above was taken at the Indian Alley, and the image below was captured under the Mare Island bridge. (Both, courtesy of Jaime Esparza.)

The Vallejo Naval & Historical Museum is a 501(c)(3) nonprofit organization. It preserves and exhibits the diverse and exciting history of the city of Vallejo and the former US Naval Shipyard at Mare Island. The museum is located in Vallejo's historic Old City Hall and features five galleries devoted to community and US Navy history.

Consistent with our mission to preserve history on a local level, this book was printed in South Carolina on American-made paper and manufactured entirely in the United States. Products carrying the accredited Forest Stewardship Council (FSC) label are printed on 100 percent FSC-certified paper.